engage

Welcome to the second issue of engage, the brand new Bible notes that will be bursting into the world every three months, grabbing you by the eyeballs and plunging you straight into God's life-changing word. In this issue...

✱ DAILY READINGS — each day's page throws you into the Bible, to get you handling, questioning and exploring God's message to you. And it encourages you to act on it and talk to God more in prayer.

THIS ISSUE: follow Abraham's footsteps in **Genesis**; follow the signs to discover the real Jesus in **John**; follow the garbage trail with **Habakkuk**; follow the building plans in **Haggai** and follow Paul's brilliant advice in **1 Timothy**.

✱ TAKE IT FURTHER — if you're left wanting more at the end of an engage page, turn to the '*Take it further*' section to dig deeper.

✱ STUFF — articles on stuff relevant to young Christians. This time the topic is **money**.

✱ TRICKY — tackling some of those mind-bendingly tricky questions that confuse us all, as well as questions that our friends bombard us with. This issue: **How do we know God exists?**

✱ ESSENTIAL — articles on the basics we really need to know about God, the Bible and Christianity. This time we focus on **God the Father** — what makes Him a Dad?

✱ REAL LIVES — amazing true stories, revealing God at work in people's lives. This time — the trials of life in a non-Christian family.

✱ TOOLKIT will give you the tools to help you wrestle with the Bible and understand it for yourself. This issue we ask: **What's the point?**

All of us who work on engage are passionate to see God's word at work in people's lives. Do you want God's word to have an impact on your life? Then open your Bible, and start on the first engage study right now...

HOW TO USE engage

1 Set a time you can read the Bible every day

2 Find a place where you can be quiet and think

3 Grab your Bible, pen and a notebook

4 Ask God to help you understand what you read

5 Read the day's verses with **engage** taking time to think about it

6 Pray about what you have read

BIBLE STUFF We use the NIV Bible version, so you might find it's the best one to use with **engage**. If the notes say **'Read Haggai 2 v 8–10'**, look up Haggai in the contents page at the front of your Bible. It'll tell you which page Haggai starts on. Find chapter 2 of Haggai, and then verse 8 of chapter 2 (the verse numbers are the tiny ones). Then start reading!

In this issue...

ENGAGE LINE-UP

Writers: Martin Cole Cassie Martin Jill Silverthorne Jim Overton
Tim Thornborough Helen Thorne

Editor: Martin Cole

Design dreamer: Steve Devane

Publishing bigwig: Tim Thornborough

Eagle eyes: Anne Woodcock

Promises Promises

Lies, deception, war, daring rescues, surprising babies, angels in disguise, circumcision (ouch!), child sacrifice (almost!), incest, a woman turned into a salt stack, and evil cities destroyed by burning sulphur — it's all in Genesis 12–25.

NEW BEGINNINGS

There are some incredible stories here in Genesis, but at the heart of it all, we meet an awesome God in control. If Genesis 1–11 was about the beginning of the human race, then chapters 12–25 are about the beginning of the people of God. We meet Abraham — a man faithful to God — and his, er, *interesting* family. And we see how they fit into God's plans for a nation ruled by Him.

PROMISES PROMISES

In Genesis 12–25, God makes amazing promises to Abraham and his family (who would become God's chosen people, the Israelites). The promises God makes here in Genesis are kept throughout the whole of the Bible. And they ultimately come true through Jesus. Even at the beginning of the Bible, we're pointed to Jesus Christ!

REVEALING STUFF

In the Bible, God reveals Himself to His people in stages, gradually showing them more about Himself, building on what He's already taught them. Through His promises to Abraham, we begin to see more of what God's like and His incredible plans for His people.

If you want great stories, you've come to the right place. But delve a little deeper, and you'll also see the incredible, powerful, loving God behind it all.

OK, take it away, Abraham. Or should that be Abram...?

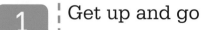

1 | Get up and go

Some stories are slow to start, gradually building an atmosphere. Not so with Abram. We're thrown straight into the middle of things, with God giving Abram mind-boggling orders and promises straightaway...

👁 Read Genesis 12 v 1–5

ENGAGE YOUR BRAIN

▷ *What did God command Abram to do?*
▷ *Why was it hard for Abram? (v1)*
▷ *But what amazing promises did God make?*

God suddenly told Abram to leave his home and his people and step into the unknown. Abram trusted God to guide him and took his family on this mysterious adventure (v4–5). And the Lord made some history-shaping promises to Abram...

Promise 1 — Children
Abram's family would grow into a great nation (v2). But look back at Genesis 11 v 29–30: Abram was 75 and his wife Sarai couldn't have kids. God's first promise looked unlikely.

Promise 2 — Blessing
Through Abram, God would bless everyone on the planet (v3). Again, it seems improbable. But the rest of

the Bible shows us that **Jesus** was a descendant of Abram. It was Jesus who would be a blessing to the whole world.

👁 Read verses 6–9
▷ *What new promise did God make? (v7)*

Promise 3 — Land
The Lord promised to give the whole land of Canaan to Abram's descendants. Another unlikely promise, but Abram believed God.

Christians have the Bible and know Jesus. Abram had neither and yet was prepared to trust God and step into an unknown future.
▷ *How is he an example to you?*

PRAY ABOUT IT

Thank God for His awesome promises. Pray that, like Abram, you'll trust and obey God.

→ TAKE IT FURTHER
Leave this behind for page 108.

2 | Who do you trust?

You're in a tight spot. You fear for the worst and you don't know what to do. Do you trust your own instincts? Phone a friend? Or maybe even turn to God for help?

👁 **Read Genesis 12 v 10-16**

ENGAGE YOUR BRAIN

▶ *What did Abram do when famine hit the land? (v10)*

▶ *What did he do when he feared for his safety? (v11-13)*

▶ *How many times is God mentioned in verses 10-16?*

Abram was living in Canaan, the place God led him to. But when famine struck, Abram didn't seek God's help — he ran off to Egypt. And when he feared the Egyptians might kill him and take Sarai, Abram told a half-truth (Sarai was his half-sister) to save his skin.

God isn't mentioned in these verses because Abram didn't turn to the Lord for help. He tried to sort his problems out by himself. It's always a big mistake to tackle a problem without asking God's help.

👁 **Read verses 17–20**

Because of Abram's lies, Sarai became Pharaoh's wife, God gave Pharaoh serious diseases, and Abram and Sarai were thrown out of the country. Yet God was still with them!

It's so easy to take matters into our own hands. We sometimes trust ourselves more than we trust God. But because of Jesus, we can turn to God for help in living His way.

PRAY ABOUT IT
Tell God about difficult situations you're facing at the mo. Ask Him to help and guide you.

THE BOTTOM LINE
Trust God, not yourself.

→ **TAKE IT FURTHER**
Trust me, if you want more, you should turn to page 108.

3 | Time to split

Abram had made a mess of things in Egypt by not turning to God for guidance. But, amazingly, God was still with him and his family. So, would Abram learn from his mistakes?

👁 Read Genesis 13 v 1–4

ENGAGE YOUR BRAIN
ⓘ *What did Abram do this time? (v4)*

That's a good pattern to follow: when you've done wrong, go quickly back to God. Talk to Him, ask Him to guide you.

Abram's back trusting God, but how will he react when he's tested again?

👁 Read verses 5–13

ⓘ *What was the problem? (v7)*

ⓘ *How did Abram deal with it? (v8–9)*

ⓘ *How wise was Lot's choice? (v12–13)*

Abram and his nephew Lot had become so rich that the land wasn't big enough for both of them and their families and animals. Abram had the right to choose who farmed where because he was top man in the family. But he showed great generosity by letting Lot choose. Lot chose perfect farming land, near the river Jordan. But it was near the sin-infested city of Sodom. Later on, we'll see what a bad move this was.

GET ON WITH IT
ⓘ *How can you be more generous with people around you? List three specific things you can do:*

•

•

•

PRAY ABOUT IT
Ask the Lord to remind you to do those things. And bring any problems or decisions you have to God, asking Him to guide you.

→ TAKE IT FURTHER

Peace be with you... on page 108.

4 ┆ Showing promise

In the best thrillers, the plot is revealed slowly. Bit by bit, we're given new facts, until we can start to piece together what's happening. Things gradually start to make sense.

God made three great promises to Abram (Genesis 12 v 1–7). Gradually, the Lord reveals more and more about these incredible promises. And He also reveals more about Himself.

👁 Read Genesis 13 v 14–18

ENGAGE YOUR BRAIN

▶ *What does God reveal about His promise of land? (v14–15)*

▶ *And what about the promise of children? (v16)*

▶ *How does the Lord get Abram to appreciate His promises? (v17)*

God is so good to His people and treats them far better than they could imagine! God revealed to Abram just how amazing His promises were — Abram's family would become a huge nation (v16), and they would have this great land, as far as the eye could see (v15).

Throughout the Bible, we gradually begin to see how awesome, loving, forgiving and powerful our God is. He gives us far more than we could ever deserve or imagine. Sending His Son to die for us was the ultimate example of this.

GET ON WITH IT
Abram walked around the country, taking in all that God had promised to give him.
▶ *What can you do to make sure you appreciate the great things God has given you?*

PRAY ABOUT IT
Thank God for some of the specific things He's given you. Ask Him to reveal more and more of Himself to you as you read your Bible.

THE BOTTOM LINE
God is so good to His people!

➔ TAKE IT FURTHER
For more of God's promises, wander over to page 108.

5 | Lot of trouble

Remember how Abram let his nephew Lot have first choice of where to live? Lot chose great farming land, but it was near Sodom, where people sinned against God in disgusting ways.

Keep that at the back of your brain. But first, a big battle between loads of kings with crazy names...

👁 Read Genesis 14 v 1–12

ENGAGE YOUR BRAIN

▶ *Where was Lot living before? (Genesis 13 v 12)*

▶ *Where's he living now? (Genesis 14 v 12)*

Four powerful kings attacked five cities (including Sodom) on the plain of Jordan. By now, Lot had moved into the evil city. What a bad move!

GET ON WITH IT

▶ *Is there anywhere you go or people you hang out with that tempt you away from living God's way?*
▶ *What will you do about it?*

Lot was kidnapped along with all his possessions. Time for Abram to come to the rescue...

👁 Read verses 13–16

▶ *How was Abram able to rescue Lot so successfully? (see v20)*

With the help of his allies and some cunning night-time tactics, Abram made a successful attack and rescued Lot. Nice work. But it was God who was behind Abram's victory.

PRAY ABOUT IT

Thank God that He's in control. Spend time thanking God for specific things He's enabled you to do.

THE BOTTOM LINE

God's behind the good stuff.

→ TAKE IT FURTHER

For extra advice on right living, run to page 109.

Two for one offer

Know anyone who's got two jobs? Waiter and actor. Teacher and mother. Taxi driver and ballet dancer. Today, Abram meets a man who has two seriously important jobs...

👁 Read Genesis 14 v 17–20

ENGAGE YOUR BRAIN

▶ *What two impressive roles did Melchizedek have? (v18)*

▶ *What did he recognise about Abram's victory? (v20)*

Not only did Melkich...Meldizzy... Milkyway... this king/priest have two great jobs and say some great things to Abram, he also reminds us of someone else.

▶ *Any ideas who?*

The book of Hebrews tells us that Melchizedek reminds us of Jesus. Jesus is king and priest. He's the **King over everything** and He was the **ultimate priest** because, when He died and rose again, He took away the sins of God's people. Stunning.

👁 Read verses 21–24

▶ *How did the king of Sodom want to divide the people and things Abram had captured?*

▶ *What's Abram's surprising answer?*

Usually the reward for winning a battle was to keep everything (and everyone) you captured. But Abram refused to keep anything the king of Sodom gave him. He wanted people to know that everything he had came from God. And he gave a tenth of his possessions back to God too (v20).

GET ON WITH IT

Everything you have comes from God.

▶ *What can you give back to Him? Time? Money? Possessions?*

▶ *How exactly will you do that?*

PRAY ABOUT IT

You must have loads to thank God for today, and a few things to ask Him.

THE BOTTOM LINE

Everything we have comes from God.

→ TAKE IT FURTHER

For the lowdown on Melchizedek and Jesus, go to page 109.

7 | Game of two halves

What promises had God made to Abram? Flick back through engage **if your brain has frozen. Today, we'll see God confirm those promises in a spectacular way.**

👁 Read Genesis 15 v 1–6

ENGAGE YOUR BRAIN

▶ *What was Abram worried about? (v2–3)*

▶ *How did God answer Abram and encourage him? (v5, v1)*

▶ *What was Abram's response? (v6)*

The Lord said He would protect Abram. In fact, having God with him was Abram's greatest reward (v1). Yet Abram still doubted God's promise to give him a huge family. So God said *'Go count the stars — that's the number of offspring you'll have!'*

Abram believed and trusted God (v6). It's one of the brilliant moments in the Bible. For us, too — as we trust God to forgive us by what Jesus has done, He counts us right with God.

▶ *How does your life show that you trust God?*

👁 Read verses 7–21

▶ *What would you say is happening here? Any ideas?*

Abram wanted to be sure that God would keep His promises. So the Lord reminded Abram of how He'd been faithful in the past (v7) and would be in the future (v14–16).

God made a covenant (agreement) with Abram. When making a covenant, two people would sacrifice animals and walk between the bodies. If you broke the agreement, you'd be cut to pieces too. Ouch. The fire pot and torch were a sign that God was there, making this promise.

PRAY ABOUT IT

God has promised to forgive His people and keep them safe forever. He always keeps His promises. Spend a while praising and thanking God.

→ TAKE IT FURTHER

For the second half, try page 109.

8 You've got Ishmael

How good are you at waiting? Are you really patient, or do you tear your hair out when you're waiting for stuff? It had been 10 years since God promised Abram and Sarai a son...

👁 Read Genesis 16 v 1–6

ENGAGE YOUR BRAIN

▶ *How would you describe Sarai's feelings?*

▶ *What happened because of Sarai's and Abram's impatience and failure to trust God?*

Abram and Sarai gave up on God giving them the son He'd promised. They tried to fix the problem themselves, but the result was a pregnant slave girl (v4), hate (v4), blame (v5), and a runaway mum-to-be (v6).

Sometimes it defies logic to trust God's word, so we try to fix things ourselves. But God wants us to trust Him so that our faith gets stronger.

👁 Read verses 7–16

▶ *God cared for this pregnant Egyptian slave girl. What does that tell you about God?*

▶ *What did Hagar recognise about God?*

Hagar felt unloved and alone. Yet God saw her misery and cared for her. But Ishmael wasn't the son God had promised Abram. He and Sarai would have to wait a little longer.

TALK IT THROUGH

Grab a Christian friend or two and talk about...
• times you're tempted to not trust God and do things your way instead
• the consequences of doing things your way instead of God's
• how you can encourage each other to trust God and hold on to His promises

PRAY ABOUT IT

Talk to God about what's on your mind today.

THE BOTTOM LINE

Be patient and wait for God.

→ TAKE IT FURTHER

Donkey business on page 109.

Lifetime guarantee

What do you think you'll be doing in 13 years time? Will you still be walking God's way? From yesterday's story, we now jump forward 13 years with Abram. But is God still with Abe?

👁 Read Genesis 17 v 1–8

ENGAGE YOUR BRAIN
▶ *What did God promise...*
- *for Abram? (v4–5)*
- *for Abram's family? (v6, 8)*
- *for ever? (v7)*

▶ *What did God demand of Abram? (v1)*

God was definitely still with Abram. He confirmed His brilliant covenant promises again and gave Abram a few more details. He would now be called *'Abraham'* which means *'father of many'*. God promised Abraham he'd have loads of descendants, including kings. God promised to give Abraham's family the land of Canaan (they were still aliens/foreigners there at this point). The Lord promised to be their God and He would keep His promises forever!

God told Abraham to keep obeying Him and living for Him. Oh, and to do something else too...

👁 Read verses 9–14

▶ *What did Abraham's family have to do?*

▶ *Why? (v11)*

Every male had to have the foreskin around their penis cut off. Sounds weird and painful (hands up if your eyes are watering). But it was a sign of God's covenant. Like wearing a badge saying *'Hey, I'm part of God's people and He's looking after me!'* But it wasn't a ticket to heaven; you still had to trust and obey God (v1).

PRAY ABOUT IT
Read verse 1 again. Are you ready to live like that? What needs changing? Talk to God about it and ask His help.

THE BOTTOM LINE
God is brilliant to His people but they must walk His way.

➡ TAKE IT FURTHER
For more, walk over to page 109.

10 | Promise keeper

Yesterday we read about the awesome promises God made to Abraham. And God's not finished yet... But how do we know God keeps His promises?

👁 Read Genesis 17 v 15–22

ENGAGE YOUR BRAIN
Four more promises here. Find them and sum them up in your own words.

▶ *Promise 1 (v16):*

This promise came true. Whole nations were descended from Abraham and Sarah. Some of them were kings like David and Solomon.

▶ *Promise 2 (v19):*

A baby for this doddery couple? Surely not! If you want to find out what happened, flick ahead to Genesis 21 v 1–7.

▶ *Promise 3 (v20):*

It happened in Genesis 25 v 12–18.

▶ *Promise 4 (v21):*

God would have a covenant with Isaac too. His many descendants would live in Canaan, and the whole world would be blessed through a member of his family — **Jesus**.

All of these promises came true, giving us even more evidence that God keeps His promises.

👁 Read verses 23–27
Don't worry, we don't have to get circumcised these days (phew, lads!) The Bible later talks about a circumcision of the **heart** — it's our attitude He's most concerned about. God wants people to trust and obey Him. In everything.

THE BOTTOM LINE
God ALWAYS keeps His promises.

➔ TAKE IT FURTHER
To avoid the chop, try page 109.

REAL LIVES

Each month in REAL LIVES, we'll talk to people whose lives have been transformed by Christ. This issue, **Charlotte Fox** talks about life as a Christian in a non-Christian family.

How did you become a Christian?
I was brought up in a non-Christian family, living with my mum and my sister. During the summer holidays after Year 7, I started praying a bit, wanted to obey the Ten Commandments and be a nicer person, for a reason I can't explain.

In Year 8, I met my best friend who was from a Christian family, and we started going to Christian Union together. One day she rang and said she'd become a Christian. I didn't understand this as I thought she already was one, but she explained that she had given her life fully to Christ. A few days later, I did the same, and was filled with joy and a desire to serve God.

What was your family's reaction?
As I changed, my mum became more and more anti-Christian. She didn't like me reading Christian books or listening to Christian music or going to Christian events. She was always telling me how disappointed she was in me — that I was not a *'normal'* teenager who read magazines rather than the Bible. I was only allowed to go to church when the family did, every month or so, and I was not allowed to find a different church where the gospel was preached more faithfully.

What kinds of opposition to your faith have you faced at home?
A few years after I had become a Christian, my mum was clearing out my room and found lots of Christian things; she got very angry and tore up my Christian books, broke my Christian CDs and took away my Bible. From the start of the Easter holidays, I couldn't see my Christian friends or go to church, and I couldn't read my Bible or do anything *'Christian'*. They were the hardest two weeks of my life, but I realised the one thing that couldn't be taken away from me was prayer. I realised then what a precious and powerful

gift prayer is, and I had to learn to lean totally on God's strength. After a few months, I was allowed my Bible back to read just on Sundays. I'm now at univesity, but I'm still not allowed to go to church or Christian events when I'm at home.

Why didn't you just give up on God for an easy life?
When I compare my hardships to those Jesus faced, I see that they're nothing. He went through so much that I go through, including His family thinking He was *'out of his mind'* (Mark 3 v 21), but He also went through so much more. Jesus is the perfect example of perseverance, which I must strive for.

What kept you going as a Christian?
I've found it difficult to keep going despite so much opposition, but God has held me close to Him. Since starting university, I've really enjoyed the freedom I have to serve God in so many ways, particularly in my involvement with church. When I go home for the holidays, I feel discouraged, but I've realised I can also serve God there by witnessing to my family through how I act.

My mum has noticed my increased kindness, patience and willingness to help out around the house. And although she still opposes my faith, I hope that one day my witness will be used by God in her salvation. Praying for her is tough when it seems there are no results, but I know God is faithful, so I will not give up. As the Bible says: *'Do not be anxious about anything, but in everything, by prayer and petition, with thanksgiving, present your requests to God.'* (Philippians 4 v 6)

> I've found it difficult to keep going despite so much opposition, but God has held me close to Him.

How would you encourage other people in a similar situation?
'Consider it pure joy, my brothers, whenever you face trials of many kinds, because you know that the testing of your faith develops perseverance.' (James 1 v 2-3)

If you have a similar story you'd like to share with us, or need encouragement from the Bible on this subject, email engage@thegoodbook.com

John

Identity parade

If you want to find out what someone's really like, you do some research. You read books and articles about them. You google them. You gather as much info on them as you can to build a clear picture of who they are and what they're like.

THE EVIDENCE

John was writing to convince his readers about who Jesus was. In chapters 6–8 of his book, John provides us with plenty of evidence to solve the BIG mystery... who exactly is this man?

Exhibit A: Jesus shows who He is by **what He does** — two awe-inspiring miracles in chapter 6.

Exhibit B: Jesus shows who He is by **what He says**: His claims about Himself are so incredible that we can't ignore them.

DIVIDED OPINION

People who actually saw Jesus' miracles and heard His huge claims gave a variety of verdicts...

- Jesus' followers had divided opinions (John 6 v 60–71)
- Jesus' own brothers didn't believe (John 7 v 3–10)
- People who heard Jesus' words had loads of different ideas about Him (John 6 v 15, 42, John 7 v 31, 43)
- The Jewish leaders were out to kill Jesus (John 7 v 1)

And they threw the book at Him — well, the Old Testament law books anyway. The Jews went back to their traditional views of religion, rather than accepting that this man was God's chosen king (*the Christ*) sent by God to rescue His people.

THE VERDICT

John rounds off with an amazing piece of evidence at the beginning of Chapter 8. The story shows that Jesus did carry out the law — He was the only one who had never broken it! So John knows who Jesus is, but...

Who do you think Jesus really is?

11 Just for starters

Over the next few days we're going to feast on John's teaching. John's going to fill our plate with the facts about Jesus. Prepare to be well-fed — as long as you like bread...

👁 Read John 6 v 1–13

ENGAGE YOUR BRAIN

▶ Why was this huge crowd following Jesus? (v2)

▶ Why did Jesus ask Philip about buying bread? (v5–6)

▶ How did Jesus stun everyone? (v10)

Jesus and His disciples were disturbed by a hungry crowd. He knew how He'd stop their stomachs rumbling, but asked His disciples to solve the problem first. He was testing their faith. They didn't have an answer, so Jesus did some outrageous maths — dividing the bread and fish, then multiplying them to feed thousands. Nothing's impossible for Jesus.

👁 Read verses 14–15

▶ How did the crowds react to Jesus' lip-smacking miracle?

▶ Why do you think Jesus didn't hang around at the end? (v15)

Jesus knew they hadn't grasped the sort of king He was. He hadn't come to set them free from their Roman overlords. Jesus had come to be king of their **lives**, not their country. He had come to rescue them from **sin**, not from the Romans.

Jesus left His signature in this miracle. He spelt His name G-O-D, but the crowd just couldn't read it.

PRAY ABOUT IT

▶ What does Jesus mean to you?
▶ Is He the King of your whole life, or just someone to look up to?

Talk to God honestly about your answers.

THE BOTTOM LINE

Nothing's impossible for Jesus. He wants to be King of your life.

➡ TAKE IT FURTHER

Still feeling hungry? Try page 110.

12 | Water break

What terrifies you? What leaves your hair standing on end and your legs turned to jelly? Spiders? The dark? Beards?

What about Jesus? Is He even slightly scary?

👁 Read John 6 v 16–24

ENGAGE YOUR BRAIN

▶ *What scared the disciples? (v19)*

▶ *What did Jesus say to them?*

▶ *Why do you think only the disciples saw this miracle?*

▶ *What did they learn from it?*

The disciples saw another amazing miracle from Jesus. It was a further sign pointing to who Jesus is. It showed that He is God and He's in control of everything, including the laws of nature.

But it wasn't the storm that freaked out the disciples. It was seeing Jesus doing the impossible — walking on water — that paralysed them with fear. Jesus' power really is terrifying. So Jesus comforted them. *'Don't be afraid'* He said. What took away their fear was realising that this powerful person was their Master and Friend.

The most common command in the Bible is **Do not be afraid**. Flick through your Bible and count how many times it's used. Just kidding. It appears 366 times — one for each day of the year in a leap year.

People should be afraid of Jesus if He's not their Master and Friend. But with Jesus on their side, Christians don't need to be afraid. They can always turn to Him when they're scared and He won't let them down. He's the King of the universe!

PRAY ABOUT IT

▶ *Is there anything you're scared or worried about?*
Share it with God, and ask Him to help you conquer your fear, trusting in Jesus.

THE BOTTOM LINE

Don't be afraid of stuff life throws at you — Jesus is much more powerful.

→ TAKE IT FURTHER

Follow the signs to page 110.

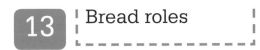

13 | Bread roles

John's feeding us the truth about Jesus. The crowd caught up with Jesus, and chewed over the miracle they'd been part of. They asked 3 questions, but Jesus went beyond the obvious answers to challenge what they really believed about Him.

ENGAGE YOUR BRAIN

Q: Read John 6 v 25
A: Read John 6 v 26–27
Jesus pointed out why the people wanted Him — so they could stuff their stomachs. But He moved the discussion from belly-filling bread to a different variety altogether — one that would never need replacing.

▶ *What kind of food is Jesus talking about?*

Q: Read John 6 v 28
A: Read John 6 v 29
The crowd missed the point: God didn't want their work, He wanted them to believe in His Son. They couldn't earn their way into God's good books with good deeds.

▶ *What's the only way to get right with God? (v29)*

Q: Read John 6 v 30-31
A: Read John 6 v 32-34
Although they'd already had a sign, the crowd wanted more! They brought up a famous bread from their history — manna — which miraculously fell from the sky and fed their ancestors in the desert. Jesus pointed out that this bread came from God. He used the idea of something coming down from heaven to introduce a different sort of bread altogether.

▶ *What, or who, is Jesus talking about in verse 33?*

God had now given them something far more important than manna or bread — He'd given them His own Son, Jesus.

PRAY ABOUT IT

Thank God that He's shown you that to please Him, you need faith in His Son. Ask Him to strengthen your faith in Jesus.

THE BOTTOM LINE

Good deeds aren't good enough. Only Jesus can give us eternal life.

→ TAKE IT FURTHER

Use your loaf... turn to page 110.

14 | Bread or alive

What food could you eat and eat and eat until you were stuffed to bursting point? John's still stuffing us with facts about Jesus, and today we come to the main course. Feast on this...

Read John 6 v 35–40

ENGAGE YOUR BRAIN

▶ How does Jesus compare Himself to hunger-satisfying bread? (v35)

▶ How do we get hold of this life-giving bread? (v35, 37, 40)

▶ Is it down to us, or is someone else behind this amazing gift? (v37–40)

All this talk of bread has left people hungry. But Jesus can satisfy real hunger — our hunger for life, for a reason to live. It's not down to us at all, it's a gift from God. All we have to do is **believe** that Jesus can satisfy our cravings.

Jot down what Jesus promises to those who trust in Him in...

Verse 37:

Verse 39:

Verse 40:

Have you taken all that in??? Jesus won't turn away *anyone* who turns to Him. He won't lose any of them. One day He will raise them up to live with Him forever. How ridiculously, mind-blowingly phenomenal is that?

PRAY ABOUT IT

If you trust in Jesus, you've got so much to thank Him for. You'd best start right now...

Sadly, not everyone believes in Jesus (v36). Pray for someone you know who hasn't accepted this amazing, life-giving gift yet. Maybe yourself?

THE BOTTOM LINE

Only Jesus can truly satisfy.

➔ TAKE IT FURTHER

Still got hunger pangs? Try page 110.

15 ¦ Flesh eaters

Yesterday Jesus claimed to be the 'bread of life'. It's a bit of a weird claim — maybe we can ignore it and move on... No chance. Jesus keeps repeating it and goes even further...

Read John 6 v 41–51

ENGAGE YOUR BRAIN

▶ *What did the Jews get wrong about Jesus? (v42)*

▶ *Who was Jesus' real father?*

▶ *How is Jesus better than manna? (v49–51)*

These people refused to believe that Jesus was God's Son. They wouldn't accept His claims as they thought He was just an ordinary guy like them. But Jesus was so much more.

Back in Exodus, God sent manna (bread from heaven) to feed the Israelites in the desert. It kept them alive, but eventually they died. But God sent Jesus from heaven into the world to give people *eternal* life.

Read verses 52-59

▶ *What did the Jews misunderstand this time? (v52)*

▶ *What do you think Jesus meant by this stomach-churning claim?*

Don't worry, Jesus wasn't saying we have to actually eat Him! Faith in Jesus is a lot like eating. You have to eat to live. And to live forever we have to trust in Jesus' death. He gave His body and blood on the cross to rescue us from sin. You have to rely fully on His death for you.

SHARE IT

Do your friends and family realise that trusting in Jesus' death is the only way to eternal life? Think of ways you can (gently and compassionately) share this vital truth with them.

TALK IT THROUGH

Discuss your ideas with Christian friends. Talk about ways you can point people to the truth about Jesus.

THE BOTTOM LINE

Only Jesus' death can give us life.

21

16 | The big choice

What do you think of Jesus' claims about Himself? Made your mind up about Him yet? Jesus had been talking with the crowds — now He's back with His followers. They were struggling with what He'd said.

👁 Read John 6 v 60-71

ENGAGE YOUR BRAIN

▶ *Why did many of Jesus' followers leave Him?*

▶ *Who was the most shocking person who would desert Him? (v70-71)*

Those who turned away couldn't stomach His teaching. Their lives would have to change too much if they lived His way. Jesus knew that these hangers-on wouldn't stick by Him when He suffered and died and went back to heaven (v62).

Many of Jesus' followers were more interested in earthly things (food, power, good deeds) than spiritual stuff. Jesus says these things count for nothing (v63). Only Jesus can give what really matters — eternal life.

▶ *What had Simon Peter understood about Jesus? (v68–69)*

▶ *Is Peter's answer yours too?*

Jesus gave everyone a choice. Some went for the wrong option and deserted Jesus, but a few proved they understood exactly who He was and chose to be His disciples. Jesus pointed out that the choice was actually two-way: they chose Him, but God had chosen them first (v65).

PRAY ABOUT IT

Ask God to help you make your mind up about Jesus. Pray that you might know for sure if you're a genuine follower of Christ. If you're not, ask God to show you who Jesus really is.

THE BOTTOM LINE

The choice is yours...

→ TAKE IT FURTHER

Will you choose to take it further? If yes, page 110. If no, page 4567.

22

17 | Wanted: Jesus Christ

In Judea, Jesus was a wanted man. He was fairly safe while He stayed in Galilee, but the Jewish leaders in Judea were out to get Him as soon as He arrived there.

👁 Read John 7 v 1–9

ENGAGE YOUR BRAIN

▶ *What did Jesus' brothers want Him to do?*

▶ *What do you think Jesus meant by 'the right time' in verse 6?*

▶ *Why did so many people hate Jesus? (v7)*

John shows us different people's reactions to Jesus. The Jewish leaders were out to kill Him, His own brothers didn't believe Him, and many people hated Him. Jesus' brothers wanted Him to go to the feast and prove who He was. But it wasn't the right time.

Jesus came to earth to die on the cross, to rescue people from their sins. But it wasn't time for His death yet. It wasn't time to walk into the traps of His killers.

👁 Read verses 10–13

▶ *What were people's different opinions of Jesus?*

▶ *What do your friends say about Jesus?*

Jesus divided the crowd. They were interested in Him, but split in their opinions. Because their leaders were having a crack-down, they daren't discuss Jesus in public, but whispered about Him secretly.

GET ON WITH IT

This week, try to find out what your friends think about Jesus. Who do they think He is? It will help you understand them a little more.

PRAY ABOUT IT

Ask the Lord to help you sensitively bring up the topic of Jesus, and find out what your friends think.

→ TAKE IT FURTHER

Wanted: You. Reward on page 111.

18 | Heaven sent

'They're giving out free TVs in the mall!'
Do you tend to believe amazing claims, or do you check where they come from? The Jewish leaders wanted to know where Jesus' amazing teaching came from...

👁 Read John 7 v 14–18

ENGAGE YOUR BRAIN

▶ *What were Jesus' listeners astonished by? (v15)*

▶ *What did Jesus remind them? (v16)*

▶ *How can we be sure that Jesus' words come from God? (v17)*

We sometimes take Jesus' words for granted. But this is God speaking to us! So we should listen up!

If we live God's way, we'll discover that Jesus' teaching really does come from God. And we'll let it have an impact on our lives.

👁 Read verses 19-24

▶ *What did people claim Jesus had done that was wrong? (Flick back to John 5 v 5–9, 16)*

▶ *What point did Jesus make? (John 7 v 23)*

▶ *What were they doing that was far worse? (v19)*

These guys claimed to keep God's law. Yet they broke God's law by wanting to kill Jesus. They thought it was okay to carry out circumcision on a Sabbath. But they thought it was terrible for Jesus to completely heal someone! Crazy!

Yet again, they'd got Jesus completely wrong. They refused to believe He was sent by God. Instead, they thought they were God's people, despite not living God's way and rejecting His Son!

PRAY ABOUT IT

I'll leave you to decide what you need to talk to God about today.

THE BOTTOM LINE

Jesus was sent by God.
Listen to Him. Obey Him.

→ TAKE IT FURTHER

For the prequel, go to page 111.

19 Check the evidence

As the feast continued, the locals found Jesus' case more and more confusing. They asked plenty of questions, but couldn't put all the bits of evidence together to come up with the right answers.

👁 **Read John 7 v 25–36**

ENGAGE YOUR BRAIN

▷ *What things did they fail to understand about Jesus? (v27, v31, v35-36)*

▷ *Why couldn't they arrest Him? (v30)*

Look at the evidence they were faced with:
• Jesus taught in public and wasn't arrested (v26)
• The idea was out there that Jesus could be the Christ — the King who would rescue them (v26–27)
• Jesus told them He was sent by God (v28–29)
• No one could arrest Jesus (v30, 32)
• Jesus said He would return to the One who sent Him — God in heaven (v33–34)

But Jesus was saying: *'You think you know me, but you don't know that it's God who sent me here. You don't*

know Him at all. I know Him, because He sent me to you.'

▷ *What did Jesus predict would happen soon? (v33–34)*

Jesus knew that He would soon be killed, rise again and then go to be with His Father God in heaven, where they wouldn't be able to follow Him. That's where Jesus is now.

PRAY ABOUT IT
Thank God for sending Jesus into the world as the great Rescuer. Praise God that Jesus is now ruling with Him in heaven. And thank Him that you can understand Jesus' amazing teaching in the Bible.

THE BOTTOM LINE
Jesus was sent by God. But many people still refuse to trust in Him.

➡ **TAKE IT FURTHER**
Follow the trail to page 111.

20 Thirst quencher

Remember what's going on? Jesus is at a big feast, where His huge claims about Himself have divided people's opinion. At the end of the ceremony was a water–pouring ceremony, which explains Jesus' big finale...

👁 Read John 7 v 37–39

ENGAGE YOUR BRAIN
▶ *What whacking great promise did Jesus make?*

Life–changing stuff. For those who really thirst to know Jesus and serve Him, He promises *'streams of living water'*. Jesus is talking about the Holy Spirit. When Jesus went back to heaven, He gave His Spirit to live in the lives of all believers, helping them to live for God. What a fantastic gift.

👁 Read verses 40–44
▶ *What different responses did people have towards Jesus?*

▶ *What didn't they know about Him? (v42)*

Some people thought that Jesus was the Prophet mentioned by Moses (Deuteronomy 18 v 15). Some thought He was the Christ —the King who would rescue God's people (they were right!). Others said He couldn't be the Christ as He didn't come from Bethlehem. (They were wrong — Jesus *was* born in Bethlehem, and was even from King David's family.)

GET ON WITH IT
People have all kinds of ideas about who Jesus is. But now it's your turn to decide:
▶ *Who do YOU believe Jesus is?*

▶ *So what effect should that have on your life?*

PRAY ABOUT IT
Talk to God honestly about your answers.

THE BOTTOM LINE
Sooner or later we all have to make a decision about Jesus.

→ TAKE IT FURTHER
Thirsty for more?
Drink it in on page 111.

21 | Stand up, speak out

Has anyone ever made you feel stupid because of your beliefs? Tried to belittle you and the things that are important to you? How did it make you feel?

👁 **Read John 7 v 45–49**

ENGAGE YOUR BRAIN

▶ *Why didn't the guards arrest Jesus? (v46)*

▶ *How did the Pharisees mock those who believed Jesus' words?*

The temple guards had been sent by the Pharisees to arrest Jesus. But they were so impressed by His words, they couldn't do it!

▶ *Do Jesus' words ever stop you in your tracks?*

▶ *How can you make sure you pay more attention to His teaching?*

The Pharisees claimed that only idiots fell for Jesus' words and that no religious leaders believed in Him. But they were wrong...

👁 **Read verses 50–52**

▶ *How did Nicodemus challenge the Pharisees?*

▶ *What other false claim did they make?*

It's nonsense to suggest that no man of God could come from Galilee. Jonah did! And God can use people from *any* background to serve Him!

Nicodemus was a Jewish leader who'd had a secret meeting with Jesus (John 3 v 1–21). He stood up to the bullying Pharisees, pointing out it was against Jewish law to condemn Jesus without a trial. That must have taken guts.

SHARE IT

When the pressure's on, it's easy to go along with the crowd instead of standing up for Jesus. Will you speak out for Jesus next time?

PRAY ABOUT IT

You'd better ask for some help...

➡ **TAKE IT FURTHER**

In the 'Nic' of time — page 111.

22 Sexplosive

Ever heard this saying: *'Point your finger at somebody and you've got three fingers pointing back at you'*? **The devious, scheming Jewish leaders were about to discover its meaning...**

👁 Read John 8 v 1–6

ENGAGE YOUR BRAIN

▶ *What's the woman accused of?*

▶ *What was the Jews' real motive for bringing her to Jesus?*

This woman had been caught sleeping around. Jewish law said she should be stoned to death (although they had ignored the bit about punishing the man too). So, should she be punished?

But it was all a trap. If Jesus said *'yes'*, He'd be breaking the law of the ruling Romans. If he said *'no'*, they'd roast Him for breaking Old Testament law.

👁 Read verses 7–11

▶ *What was brilliant about Jesus' answer? (v7)*

▶ *But what was His challenge to the woman? (v11)*

We can only guess what Jesus was writing on the ground. More important than that, Jesus made His accusers realise they were just as sinful as the adulteress. When they'd all slunk off, Jesus turned to the woman.

Jesus made it clear that He hated sin and that she must turn from her sinful ways. But He refused to condemn her — how great is God's forgiveness?!

PRAY ABOUT IT

We're all filthy because of sin. We all deserve to be punished. But God offers us the chance to be forgiven. Have you accepted that offer? Do you thank God for it every day?

THE BOTTOM LINE

The Lord hates sin...
but He offers us forgiveness.

➔ TAKE IT FURTHER

To take action... go to page 111.

God and the garbage

Some ridiculously talented people can make stunning works of art out of a pile of old junk. Selecting their raw materials from the scrap heap, they create something truly awesome. But if you stand too close, all you can see is rubbish. That's how life looks to Habakkuk the prophet, before he hears from God.

GARBAGE LAND

Things were bad. Really bad. God's *promised land'* had already been split in half (*Israel* to the north and *Judah* in the south) which was not exactly pretty. Then Israel got flattened. And now Judah's bursting with corruption. **2 Kings 24 v 2–4** records the ugly truth.

THE BIGGER PICTURE

Despite this series of disasters, God is still in control. God picks Habakkuk out of the junk and lets him see what God's up to. He's on the move, through time and space, and He's still on course for victory. It's scary, but beautiful.

WHY READ HABAKKUK?

Could someone make a drama from your private diaries? How about a musical?

"Oh I went to the chemist and bought some dental floss,"

"I don't like revising, it gets right up my nose…yeah"

(Add your own tune)

Something like this — only more profound — happens to Habakkuk. The weird notes in chapter 3 (v1, 3, 19) show that later generations of God's people sang his words in worship. Habakkuk's short book was not simply for one time and place… it's for us too.

Welcome to God's guide for living in 21st–century garbage. Ready for the ride?

23 | Time to rant

A national radio station runs a rant line that's open 24 hours a day. If someone dialled the number and shoved a phone in your hand, what would you complain about? What bugs you most right now?

👁 Read Habakkuk 1 v 1–3

ENGAGE YOUR BRAIN

▷ *What things does Habakkuk feel God hasn't done?*

▷ *What does he think is God's attitude towards evil?*

Habakkuk prays and nothing happens. Maybe you know how he feels. But have you ever let rip at God like that? Maybe prayer outbursts are rare because we're not sure it's right to complain.

But the Bible is full of it! Check out some examples in **Psalm 10 v 1, Psalm 13 v 1–2, Psalm 22 v 1–2**.

👁 Read verses 3–4

▷ *As he looks out at his world...*
 – what is there plenty of?
 – what's missing?

Habakkuk's prayer is not just a selfish moan-a-thon. He's bugged by God's people and the state they're in.

A nation designed to be a model of justice has ditched everything that's fair. And he can't bear to look.

PRAY ABOUT IT

▷ *With what we know of God, what might be the concerns of His heart today...*
 – for your local church?
 – for Christians in this country?

Let God's Spirit inspire some passion in your prayer! If you're worried that too much shouting might disturb the neighbours, bury your face in a pillow and go for it! Don't blame God for stuff — He's totally fair. But let Him know what's really getting to you!

THE BOTTOM LINE
It's OK to pour your feelings out to God.

→ TAKE IT FURTHER
For further ranting, try page 111.

24 | God's chosen bullies

'PREPARE TO BE AMAZED!' That sort of build–up turns most people into sceptics. 'Oh Yeah? Go on then, impress me!' But that's how God kicks off His answer to Habakkuk's complaints. And since it's God speaking, we'd better get ready for something shocking...

👁 **Read Habakkuk 1 v 5–11**

ENGAGE YOUR BRAIN

🄳 *What are the Babylonians famous for? (v6–7)*

🄳 *In what ways are they like...*
– vultures?
– the desert wind?

🄳 *What takes the place of God in their lives? (v7, 11)*

God slams the Babylonians for self-promotion. He knows they're just out to make a name for themselves.
🄳 *In what ways are you tempted to big yourself up rather than God? Be honest...*

So the Babylonians are ruthless. Nothing too shocking in that.
🄳 *But what is God going to do with them? (v6)*

Just a sec. God is going to help a nation of evil bullies to conquer His chosen nation, Israel. Could anything be more shocking?! No wonder God's people would find that hard to stomach (v5).

Face facts. God is in charge. Totally. He can do anything He wants. He can use anyone He chooses. What's brilliant is that *'All his ways are just'* (Deuteronomy 32 v 4). So we can trust Him even when we don't understand what He's doing.

PRAY ABOUT IT

🄳 *What makes you wonder what God's up to?*
– scheming cheats who get away with it?
– violent bullies growing more powerful?

Share your confusion with God and choose to trust Him today....

THE BOTTOM LINE
God's plans are shocking but perfect.

➡ TAKE IT FURTHER
Bully for you... on page 112.

25 The big issue

You're at the movies. On the screen an image flashes before you that's so hideous, you shield your eyes behind the popcorn. In fact, you feel like fleeing the cinema in disgust. We're talking totally, gut-wrenchingly repulsive.

👁 Read Habakkuk 1 v 12–13

ENGAGE YOUR BRAIN
▶ *What can't God stand?*

▶ *What questions does this raise for Habakkuk?*

FACT: God can't stand evil.
FACT: Sometimes, evil acts go unpunished.

When we know God has whiter-than-snow purity, it's hard to figure out how evil people seem to get away with so much. This gives Habakkuk major issues. In fact his book could be subtitled: *The man who dared to ask 'Why?'*.

▶ *Are you willing to bring your big questions to God?*

👁 Read verses 14–17
▶ *What do people and fish have in common? (v14)*

▶ *What do the wicked gain from catching them? (v16)*

Habakkuk vividly describes how helpless people are being slaughtered for selfish gain. *'How can this be allowed to carry on?'* he asks (v17). We might be taken aback by Habakkuk's cheek, but shouldn't we be asking the same question?

PRAY ABOUT IT
Take time now to pray for people facing injustice and oppression. Think of specific examples. Pray because it matters. Pray because you expect answers from the God who cares.

Habakkuk knows this isn't over….
Read the cliff hanger of 2 v 1.

THE BOTTOM LINE
We can ask God big big questions.

➡ TAKE IT FURTHER
Why does bad stuff happen? See what the Bible says on page 112.

26 | Waiter waiter

Ever been stood up? You arrive at the agreed meeting point first. They must be held up, so you wait. But for how long? You don't want to give up too soon, but if you stand there all night, you'll look an idiot.

👁 **Read Habakkuk 2 v 2–3**

ENGAGE YOUR BRAIN

▶ *What did God tell Habakkuk to do? (v2)*

▶ *What should he do until all is revealed? (v3)*

God's response is coming. Habakkuk has to wait. It will *'linger'*, but it won't *'delay'*. Huh? What's the difference?

The fulfilment of God's promise may take its time arriving. His people will have to wait. But it won't be late. God's timing is always perfect. He does things at *exactly* the right time.

👁 **Read verses 4–5**

▶ *The wicked might seem to be in control but what should we spot under the surface?*

▶ *What do they never experience? (v5)*

If you've ever wondered what it's like to crave world domination, here it is. It's miserable! Greed won't let you rest. You're never satisfied!

▶ *How are God's people to live differently? (v4)*

All Christians are waiters. That is, they wait for God to put things right. But it's not about hanging around and getting bored. It means living by faith. Because of what we know about the future, we take action now. We're out to please God.

GET ON WITH IT

▶ *If someone looked at your life, could they tell what you were waiting for?*

▶ *What positive action can you take to live more for God?*

→ **TAKE IT FURTHER**

If you can't wait... go to page 112.

27 A watery end

Gangsters. Criminals. The Underworld. Crime and corruption can be painted as an adrenaline-filled route to riches. If you've ever been taken in by the glamour, God's word should put that right once and for all.

Read Habakkuk 2 v 6–8

ENGAGE YOUR BRAIN

▷ *Where does Babylon's wealth come from?*

▷ *What can they expect from their former victims?*

This might not be rocket science but… crime is madness, isn't it? What are the chances of getting away with it your whole life? Surely, somewhere you'll end up paying. And then you've got God to answer to. Doesn't sound like a genius career plan, does it?

Read verses 9–14

▷ *How did their city become so impressive? (v9, 12)*

▷ *Where will hard work get them? (v13)*

▷ *What does the future hold? (v14)*

Verse 14 gives us a poetic picture of God's plan. But what's it got to do with Babylon? Well, if the final state of the universe is wall-to-wall glory for God, then a plan to increase your own power and wealth is doomed to failure. Only God deserves the glory. Babylon would be defeated.

THINK IT THROUGH

Close your eyes. Picture yourself floating on the ocean. There's nothing but deepest blue as far as the eye can see in every direction. That's how God's rule will be forever. Complete. Uninterrupted. Unmistakable. Let that feed your courage. Stick with Him. It will be worth it.

THE BOTTOM LINE

Crime doesn't pay.

→ TAKE IT FURTHER

For a little more, turn to page 113.

28 | Home-made gods

'You are what you eat'. Which is enough to put anyone off rhubarb. Others say that owners look like their dogs. Worrying for poodle keepers. If it's true you become like what you worship, these Babylonians are in trouble...

👁 **Read Habakkuk v 15–20**

ENGAGE YOUR BRAIN

▶ What actions will backfire on the Babylonians? (v15–17)

▶ Why are idols worthless? What can they not do? (v18–19)

▶ Who's the only one who deserves our worship? (v20)

It's a ludicrous idea. Bringing home your art project and then expecting it to offer you some advice, and control your destiny. But aren't we all in danger of building our lives on dumb and lifeless nonsense?

The first wrong move humans make is serving *'created things rather than their creator'*. (Romans 1 v 25)

GET ON WITH IT

Make a note in the box (top right) of things that threaten to control you but aren't God (eg: sport, relationships, work etc).

Bible heroes often went on idol-smashing missions (Judges 6 v 25–32)

▶ Is there something that you need to throw out, or to quit doing, in order to let God rule your life?
We can make excuses but maybe it's time to shut up and take action!

PRAY ABOUT IT

If you truly mean it, tell God you want Him in charge. Ask for His help in smashing any idols in your life.

THE BOTTOM LINE

There isn't room for God *and* idols in your life.

➡ **TAKE IT FURTHER**

Belt up and go to page 113.

29 | Living in the past

Mr Saunders is more than a history teacher. With his sideburns, his collection of vinyl records and his refusal to master technology, he doesn't just talk about the past. He lives in it. But maybe that's not such a bad thing.

👁 Read Habakkuk 3 v 1–7

ENGAGE YOUR BRAIN

▷ *What qualities of God were obvious in the past? (v3–4)*

▷ *How? (v5-7)*

History can seem a bit dull sometimes. But here Habakkuk sees past events come alive. He's reminded that the stunning power of God, which rescued Israel from Egypt, is still at work... and there's only one response — awe.

👁 Read verses 8–15

▷ *Do these verses remind you of an event in the Old Testament?*

▷ *Which one?*

▷ *Who benefits from God's terrifying actions? (v13)*

These dramatic images of God remind us of the exodus, when He rescued the Israelites from Egypt.

The pictures of God in these verses are frightening, yet encouraging too. He has come to rescue. As the Lord crushes His enemies in His anger, He saves His people.

Do you ever wonder if God still cares? You don't need a special sign from God. You just need to live in the glory of the past, remembering what He's done for you. Jesus died for you. If God loved us enough to sacrifice His Son, will He ever desert us?

GET ON WITH IT

Keep the past with you today. Write Romans 8 v 32 on your hand, ankle, wallet, phone, and don't be shy if it makes someone curious!

THE BOTTOM LINE

God uses His awesome power to save His people!

→ TAKE IT FURTHER

For more evil-bashing, try page 113.

30

The happy habit

Hormones. Football scores. Your bank balance. The weather. All totally unpredictable, but they can seriously affect how you feel. Are you up one minute, down the next? What are your mood swings on a typical day?

👁 **Read Habakkuk 3 v 16**

ENGAGE YOUR BRAIN

▶ *What was Habakkuk's reaction to God's voice?*

▶ *What has replaced the impatient annoyance of 1 v 2?*

One glimpse of God's power and Habakkuk wobbled. God's control of history and His unbreakable commitment to His people left Hab stunned. Nothing had changed in the nation around him, but his attitude couldn't be more different.

👁 **Read verses 17–19**

▶ *What six shortages does he imagine?*

1.

2.

3.

4.

5.

6.

▶ *Yet what is Habakkuk's reaction? (v18–19)*

GET ON WITH IT

Create your own version of Habakkuk 3 v 17. Include potential struggles with family, money, friends etc.

Though the _____
And there are no _____
Though the _____ fails
And the _____
Though there are no _____ in the _____
And no _____ in the _____

Yet I will rejoice in the Lord.

PRAY ABOUT IT

Get yourself a praise routine. It's the best habit there is. Give it a go today. It's not just about getting out the guitar. It's about making God's love and kindness your obsession.

➡ **TAKE IT FURTHER**

The last word on Habakkuk — p 114.

TRICKY

How do we know God exists?

Each issue in TRICKY, we tackle those mind–bendingly tricky questions that confuse us as all, as well as questions that friends bombard us with to catch us out. This time, **how can you possibly know that God exists?**

'How do you know there's a God?' 'What proof have you got that your God is real?' 'Show me your evidence…' It's the kind of conversation-stopper that leaves us red in the face and stuttering 'well, erm, you see, um…'

But our faith in God is based on fact, not fiction. We may not be able to prove it, but you can say enough to show that believing in God makes sense, and that a world without God makes much less sense. Below are some ideas on what to say to your friendly atheist, and some rather difficult questions to ask them back!

A SNEAKING SUSPICION

Most people think there's something out there that's bigger and more powerful than we are. Most people think or feel that something god-like exists. Romans 1 v 20 suggests that people actually know God exists, but refuse to face up to it.
Ask them: *What makes you so sure that there isn't a God?*

WHAT A WONDERFUL WORLD

The universe is an amazing place. Galaxies, people, even tiny bugs are all awesomely made. But where did they come from? Creation whispers *'God made me!'*. (Acts 14 v 17)

Ask them: *Is it really believable that the world, you and me are just one great big accident?*

THE RIGHT STUFF

Animals don't have a sense of right and wrong. Humans do. Where does it come from? If it doesn't come naturally, then it must come from somewhere else… there's God again, peeking through the cracks in our conscience!

Ask: *If we're all an accident, then there is no such thing as right or wrong or justice. The bullies win! Is that what you actually believe?*

THE GOD WHO MAKES HIMSELF KNOWN

Those arguments might lead us to believe in a God. But none of them lead us to the God of the Bible. We need God to speak to tell us what He's really like...

THE BIBLE

God isn't silent. Throughout history God has been speaking and dealing with people. The Bible is the record of these actions — it's God's word that shows us who He is and how He wants us to live (2 Timothy 3 v 16). It tells us that God is good and holy but also loves us.

Ask them: *Ever read this amazing book? Why not give it a go and weigh up the evidence. Maybe we could read it together...*

THE SON

God sent His Son into the world to show us what He is like (John 1 v 14). Look at Jesus and you see God (John 14 v 9).

Ask them: *What do you think about Jesus? Have you ever read one of the gospels and worked out what all the fuss is about?*

THE SPIRIT

Try to think how what you've discovered about God working in your life could help someone who refuses to believe God exists.

Tell them: *Your story — how you became a Christian. Think of examples of God at work in your life that you can talk about.*

THE BOTTOM LINE

It's never possible to argue someone into believing in God. We need to be prepared to answer questions (1 Peter 3 v 15), but in the end **God** must change their hearts so they believe. God's Spirit helps people believe as they read the Bible (1 Corinthians 2 v 14). We can pray for people we know, asking God to help them believe He really does exist.

Ask them: *Dare you pray 'the doubters prayer' and mean it? 'God, if you're there, please reveal yourself to me through Jesus. And if you do, I'll follow you for the rest of my life.'*

31 | Genesis — Promises promises

You're watching TV when the doorbell rings.
You reluctantly get up to answer it — and gasp.
It's God. Nowadays we meet God as we read the Bible.
But Abraham actually met God at his front door.

👁 Read Genesis 18 v 1–8

ENGAGE YOUR BRAIN

▶ How did Abraham react to getting surprise visitors? (v2)

▶ What did Abraham do for his guests?

Abraham must have realised he had three pretty special visitors — God (v10) and two of His angels (more on the two angels in a couple of days). Abraham gave the Lord great respect (v2) and begged Him to stick around before preparing a slap-up dinner.

▶ Do you go out of your way to show people friendship?

▶ What about God? How do you treat Him?

▶ How can you give Him the respect He deserves?

👁 Read verses 9–15

▶ What surprise did God have up His sleeve? (v10)

▶ Why do you think Sarah reacted the way she did? (v11-12)

▶ What should Sarah have remembered? (v14)

Remember God's great promises to Abraham (Genesis 12 v 1–3)? Sarah thought she was far too old and wrinkly to have kids! But nothing is impossible for God. If He promised it, then it *would* happen — no matter how unlikely it seemed. Sarah also learned that we can't hide anything from God (v15).

PRAY ABOUT IT

Nothing's too hard for God, so stop putting limits on your prayers. Bring some BIG things before God right now, knowing that nothing is impossible for Him.

→ TAKE IT FURTHER

More on prayer on page 114.

32 | God in conversation

Ever begged for anything? Maybe pleaded with your parents for something you desperately wanted? Or begged your brother to stop bugging you? Abraham pleaded with God for people's lives.

👁 Read Genesis 18 v 16–19

The Lord and His two angels were about to leave Abraham. But Abraham was God's friend and his descendants would be God's chosen people. So God wanted to share with Abe what He was about to do.

It wasn't good news...

👁 Read verses 20–33

ENGAGE YOUR BRAIN

▶ *What was God going to do?*

▶ *Remember who's living in Sodom? (Genesis 14 v 12)*

▶ *As he pleads for any godly people in Sodom, what did Abraham remember about God? (v25)*

▶ *And about himself? (v27)*

God was going to see if Sodom and Gomorrah were as disgustingly sinful as was claimed. If so, they'd

be destroyed. Fair enough. Just one problem — Abraham's nephew Lot and his family were living there.

Abraham pleaded with God to save Sodom, so that the godly people there (like Lot) wouldn't be destroyed too. You can sense how desperate he was becoming to save Lot, as the numbers he asked for got smaller and smaller. He knew that God is completely fair — brilliantly, God agreed to Abraham's requests.

PRAY ABOUT IT

Thank God that He's the *'Judge of all'* and is totally fair. Think of people you desperately want God to save. Will you plead with God for them? Will you keep pleading, every day?

THE BOTTOM LINE

God's the Judge, yet He listens to our cries.

➡ TAKE IT FURTHER

Find a friend on page 114.

41

33 Lot in a hot spot

**God was going to destroy the evil city of Sodom.
But Abraham pleaded with God to save his nephew Lot.
So God sent two angels to check out the sinful city.**

Read Genesis 19 v 1–11

ENGAGE YOUR BRAIN

▷ How would you describe the people of Sodom?

▷ What did Lot do right? (v1-3, 6-7)

▷ What did he get wrong? (v8)

▷ How did God rescue Lot? (v10-11)

Sodom's inhabitants were evil and depraved. No wonder God was offended by their actions. They deserved destruction. Lot was right (and brave) to stand up to the mob.

When people around us are going against God, it's good (though really hard) to try and talk them out of it. Even when we know they'll probably ignore us, it's good to make a stand.

But Lot stuffed up by offering his own daughters to this sex-crazed gang. How could he? Lot had made a bad choice by moving into this evil city. It had clearly corrupted him, and now look at the mess he was in. Having the wrong circle of friends can affect us more than we think.

GET ON WITH IT

▷ How are you affected by the people around you?

▷ Any bad habits you've got into?

▷ What do you need to make a stand about?

PRAY ABOUT IT

Spend time thinking about this issue, bringing these things to God in prayer.

THE BOTTOM LINE

Check your surroundings.

→ TAKE IT FURTHER

What does the Bible say about homosexuality? Go to page 114.

34 Word of warning

You wake up in the middle of the night to hear someone screaming *'THE HOUSE IS ON FIRE! QUICK, GET OUT!'* **You're sooooo comfy in your bed, but it would be madness to ignore the alarm bells.**

👁 Read Genesis 19 v 12–16

ENGAGE YOUR BRAIN

▶ *What was God's verdict on the city of Sodom? (v13)*

▶ *What big mistake did Lot's in-laws make?*

▶ *Lot hesitated too, but how did God show him mercy? (v16)*

Lot's sons-in-law ignored his warnings, the idiots. And today, people ignore God's warnings to turn away from sin and avoid His punishment. God shows His great mercy to us, sending His Son to rescue us. But if we keep ignoring His warnings, we'll face destruction too.

👁 Read verses 17–29

▶ *How did God again show His mercy to Lot? (v21)*

▶ *What big mistake did Lot's wife make? (v17, 26)?*

Maybe Lot's wife couldn't bear to leave Sodom. Or maybe she doubted God. Whatever the reason, she disobeyed God, and paid the price.

God hates sin. That's why He punished Lot's wife and why He destroyed evil Sodom and Gomorrah. And yet God showed great love and mercy too. He remembered His promise to Abraham and rescued Lot.

TALK IT THROUGH

▶ *What does this story tell us about*
  – what God is like?
  – the way people treat Him?
  – what our response to God should be?

PRAY ABOUT IT

Praise and thank God that He deals fairly with sin. Thank Him for warning us and giving us many more chances to escape than we deserve.

→ TAKE IT FURTHER

Don't look back; turn to page 114.

43

35 What a mess

Why is it that just after we've experienced God's grace in an amazing way, we go and mess things up? God rescued Lot and his daughters from Sodom's destruction. But then...

👁 Read Genesis 19 v 30–38

ENGAGE YOUR BRAIN

▶ Why did Lot's daughters do what they did? (v31–32)

▶ Was Lot innocent in all this?

▶ Do you think good or bad came out of it? (v37–38 give us a clue)

Continuing the family line was a big big thing in those days. It was shameful if you had no children. So it's understandable how Lot's girls talked themselves into doing it. But that doesn't make it right. The Bible is clear that sex belongs only within marriage.

▶ What things do you persuade yourself it's OK to do, but know deep down dishonour God?

Lot wasn't innocent either. His daughters got him drunk, but it was his responsibility to look after his body. Too much alcohol can cloud our judgement or leave us vulnerable and open to sin. (More on alcohol in *Take it further* on page 114.)

👁 Read 1 Samuel 14 v 47

The descendants of Lot and his daughters became enemies of Israel, and enemies of God (Numbers 25 v 1–3 is another nasty example).

Straight after a spiritual high, we can let our guard down and let God down. When that happens, there's no point wallowing in it. We need to say sorry to God, thank Him for His forgiveness, and get back to living His way.

PRAY ABOUT IT

The issues raised today must have left you with loads to say to God...

➔ TAKE IT FURTHER

For a booze cruise — page 114.

36 | Old habits die hard

**Do you learn from your mistakes?
Or is there something you just keep getting wrong?
How do you feel when you know you've done that
same stupid thing yet again?**

👁 Read Genesis 20 v 1–2

ENGAGE YOUR BRAIN

▷ *What was Abraham's mistake?*

▷ *Why do you think he lied?*

Abraham was worried that
Abimelech would kill him and
take Sarah for himself, so he lied.
But he'd made this mistake once
before (Genesis 12 v 11–13).

👁 Read verses 3–18

▷ *What problems did Abraham's
lies cause Abimelech?*

▷ *Yet what did God call Abraham?
(v7)*

▷ *Who had Abraham trusted in
this situation — God or himself?*

Abraham had deceived Abimelech
out of fear and because he hadn't
trusted God to protect him. It's easy
to rely on our wits rather than turning
to God for help.

Yet He's in control of everything —
who better could we turn to?!

Despite Abraham messing up again,
God called him a prophet! He's the
first person in the Bible to be given
that honour — God's messenger.
God doesn't turn His back on His
people when they let Him down.
He's with them... forever.
(Check out John 5 v 24.)

PRAY ABOUT IT

▷ *What sin do you keep falling
into?*

Talk honestly with God about it. Ask
Him to help you fight it, and to trust
in Him and not your own abilities.
Thank Him that, despite repeatedly
messing up, He's still there for you.

THE BOTTOM LINE

Rely on God, not your own abilities.

→ TAKE IT FURTHER

To make a prophet, try page 115.

45

37 | Abe's babe

'Expect the unexpected'. That's an oxymoron — a statement that seems to contradict itself (like 'genuine imitation', 'pretty ugly' and 'Fun Run'). But it's a good phrase for Abraham and Sarah.

👁 Read Genesis 21 v 1–2

ENGAGE YOUR BRAIN
▶ *What does this tell us about...*
- *– God's character?*
- *– God's promises?*
- *– God's timing?*

Sarah had laughed at the idea of having a baby in her 90s. But God was gracious. As always. He kept His *'impossible'* promise. As always. His timing was perfect. As always.

👁 Read verses 3–7
▶ *How did Abraham respond to God's incredible gift to them?*

▶ *What about Sarah?*

God kept His promise; now it was Abraham's turn. He gave his son the name *'Isaac'* (it means *'he laughs'*) as God had told him to (Genesis 17 v 19). And he kept his promise to circumcise Isaac, to show that his whole family belonged to God.

Sarah had laughed mockingly at the notion of having a son. But now she laughed with *joy* at what God had done for her. God is so gracious to His people, especially when they least deserve it.

▶ *When God answers your prayers, how do you react?*

▶ *Do you even notice?*

GET ON WITH IT
On scrap paper, list some of the things God has done for you in your life.

PRAY ABOUT IT
Spend time going through your list, thanking God that He gives you far more than you could ever deserve.

THE BOTTOM LINE
God is full of grace, and always keeps His promises.

➡ TAKE IT FURTHER
Ode to joy — page 115.

38 | Outcast outcry

God kept His promise. Sarah had a baby when she was nearly 100 years old! Everyone was over the moon when Isaac was born. Well, nearly everyone...

👁 **Read Genesis 21 v 8–16**

ENGAGE YOUR BRAIN

▶ *What was the problem?*

▶ *What was God's solution? (v12)*

▶ *Yet what did God promise Hagar and Ishmael? (v13)*

Isaac was the son God had promised Abraham. It was through Isaac and his descendants (the Israelites) that God would bless the whole world.

Abraham hadn't trusted God to give him a son with Sarah, so he took matters into his own hands and slept with Hagar. Ishmael was the result. But he wasn't the son God had promised. So Abraham sent Hagar and Ishmael away. Yet God promised to make Ishmael's family into a big nation (v13). So why is He letting them die in the desert??? (v14–16)

👁 **Read verses 17–21**

▶ *What amazing things happened? (v17-19)*

▶ *What was the most amazing part for Ishmael the outcast? (v20)*

God kept His promise to Hagar and Ishmael. Even though Ishmael wasn't the son God had promised Abraham, God still cared for him.

SHARE IT
God cares for everyone, no matter what their background.
▶ *Who do you know who's a bit of an outcast?*
▶ *How could you talk to them about God's love for them?*

PRAY ABOUT IT
Thank God that He sent Jesus to the **whole world**. Pray for people you know who are outsiders. If you dare, ask God to give you opportunities to get to know them better.

➡ **TAKE IT FURTHER**
Time to cry... on page 115.

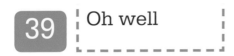

39 | Oh well

What do you find hardest about being a Christian surrounded by people who aren't interested in God? Abraham lived in a land where God wasn't worshipped. But he still had to live with those people...

👁 Read Genesis 21 v 22–24

ENGAGE YOUR BRAIN

▶ *Remember where you've seen Abimelech before? (Genesis 20)*

▶ *What did he notice about Abraham? (v22)*

Abraham had brought trouble upon Abimelech when he pretended that Sarah was his sister. But Abimelech had shown great kindness to him. And now Abimelech wants Abraham to promise that he'd do the same and treat Abimelech's family fairly. (v23).

👁 Read verses 25-34

▶ *What might have caused a fight between the two? (v25)*

▶ *How did Abraham make peace? (v27–30)*

Where Abraham lived, water was rare and often the cause of conflicts. Abraham had been wronged when Abimelech's servants seized his well.

But to avoid a fight, he struck a peace deal and even gave Abimelech gifts!

In life, we're often faced with conflicts or people treating us unfairly. As God's people, Christians must act in a way that brings Him honour. Sometimes that means compromise or even showing kindness when we've been wronged.

GET ON WITH IT

▶ *What conflicts do you need to sort out peacefully?*

▶ *What will you do to show kindness and sort things out?*

PRAY ABOUT IT

You know what you need to do...

THE BOTTOM LINE

God's people need to live God's way in a godless world.

➔ TAKE IT FURTHER

A little bit more on page 115.

40 | The toughest test

What's the hardest choice you've made this week? Which socks to wear? What to get your sister for her birthday? Maybe even a choice that affects your future? Abraham was about to face the toughest choice of his long life...

👁 **Read Genesis 22 v 1–2**

ENGAGE YOUR BRAIN

▶ *What did God command?*

▶ *Why? (v1)*

▶ *How do you think Abraham felt?*

Abraham was used to making sacrifices. He would kill an animal or bird, cook it and offer it to God. It was the way God's people said *'sorry'* or *'thank you'* to the Lord.

Abraham had waited so long to have a son and now he was being asked to sacrifice him! Shocking. God was testing Abraham. Did he really trust God? Did he love the Lord more than his own son?

👁 **Read verses 3-10**

▶ *How did Abraham show his trust in God? (v5, 8)*

▶ *Was he really prepared to sacrifice his own son for God? (v10)*

Incredible stuff. God had asked the unthinkable of Abraham. Imagine Abraham's thoughts on the three-day trip. Yet Abraham picked up the knife to kill Isaac. He showed that he loved and trusted God more than anything. He clearly loved Isaac, but God came first.

God tests our trust, too, to make it genuine and strong. To make us more like Jesus, who trusted and obeyed God fully. How does He test us? By calling us, as we read the Bible, to obey Him whatever the cost. When it goes against logic and our feelings. And He'll be there to see us through.

PRAY ABOUT IT

Ask the Lord to strengthen your faith in Him and to help you last the course even when it's tough.

THE BOTTOM LINE

Our faith is revealed in our actions.

➡ **TAKE IT FURTHER**

Trust me; turn to page 115.

41 | In the nick of time

Yesterday we ended with a cliffhanger.
Abraham had a knife poised, ready to kill his son Isaac.
Would God really make him go through with it?

👁 Read Genesis 22 v 9–14

ENGAGE YOUR BRAIN

▶ *What did God find out about Abraham? (v12)*
▶ *What did Abraham find out about God? (v14)*

The Lord stopped Abraham from killing Isaac. God saw that Abraham really did love Him and trust Him above anything else. He wouldn't hold anything back from God, not even his own son.

But the sacrifice still had to be made. So God provided a sheep to take Isaac's place. Later on in the Bible, John the Baptist said that the *'Lamb of God'* would *'take away the sin of the world'* (John 1 v 29). The Lamb of God is Jesus.

God gave Abraham a ram to take Isaac's place. And He gives us Jesus to take our place. We deserve to be punished for our sins. But God sent Jesus to die in our place.

👁 Read verses 15–19

▶ *How did God encourage Abraham?*

God mentioned His three great promises again:
1. Abraham would have loads of descendants (v17)
2. God would give them a land to live in (v17)
3. The whole world would be blessed through Abraham's descendants (v18). This last promise was fulfilled when God sent His only Son, Jesus, into the world as a blessing for the whole world. He died so that we can be forgiven.

PRAY ABOUT IT

Anything you want to thank and praise God for?

THE BOTTOM LINE

God provides. God provided His own Son to be sacrificed in our place.

➡ TAKE IT FURTHER

To dig deeper, go to page 116.

42 | Tomb with a view

Are you a trusting person?
Have you got trust issues?
Can you be trusted?
How much do you trust in God?

Read Genesis 23 v 1–15

ENGAGE YOUR BRAIN

▷ *What did Abraham want? (v8–9)*

▷ *What's Ephron's generous-sounding offer? (v11)*

▷ *But how much did he really want for the field? (v15)*

Devastating news for Abraham: Sarah died at the grand old age of 127. He wanted to buy some land so he could bury her. At first it seemed that Ephron was being hugely generous, but it was all a show. When pressed to name a price, he claimed it was worth 400 shekels (4.5kg) of silver. What a rip-off.

▷ *Are you ever crafty like that?*

▷ *Ever help people out only so you can get something out of it?*

▷ *Or maybe you're not entirely honest with your friends?*

Read verses 16–20

▷ *Why did Abraham want Sarah to be buried in Canaan rather than where they both came from?*

Remember God's three big promises to Abraham? *(See yesterday's page.)* One was that God would give Abraham's family the whole land of Canaan. Well, he's just bought his first plot of land there.

It was a small start, but Abraham buried Sarah in Canaan, trusting that one day God would give his descendants the whole land. That's full-on faith.

PRAY ABOUT IT

Ask God to help you trust Him and His promises much more. Tell Him about times you've been less than honest with people. Ask God to help you be more generous and genuine.

→ TAKE IT FURTHER

No *take it further* today, so more time to pray.

43 Thigh will be done

If someone said to you, 'Put your hand under my thigh', how would you react? Give them a funny look? Slap them hard? Let's see what Abraham's servant did...

👁 Read Genesis 24 v 1–9

ENGAGE YOUR BRAIN

▷ *What did Abraham get his servant to promise?*

▷ *Why didn't he want Isaac to marry a girl from Canaan?*

▷ *How did Abraham again show his trust in God? (v7)*

Abraham didn't want Isaac to marry anyone outside of his family — God's chosen people. He also didn't want Isaac to leave Canaan, the land God had promised to give Abraham's descendants. This meant so much to Abraham, he made his servant swear an oath. Putting his hand in a very, er, personal place showed how serious a promise it was.

Yet again, Abraham showed how much he trusted the Lord. He knew God would lead his servant to find the perfect wife for Isaac (v7).

👁 Read verses 10–16

▷ *What did the servant ask God?*

▷ *How soon did God answer?*

Now that's prayer in action! God answered before this guy had even finished talking! Sometimes God answers lightning fast, and other times we have to wait and keep praying. Notice how the servant didn't go wandering around for days, looking for the right girl. He asked God to help and show kindness to Abraham. And God did just that.

PRAY ABOUT IT

▷ *How do you need God's help?*
▷ *Who would you love God to show kindness to?*
So what are you waiting for?

THE BOTTOM LINE

Bring your requests to God. He's listening.

→ TAKE IT FURTHER

Any last requests? Go to page 116.

44 She's the one

What prayers have you seen answered recently? Have you got a long and exciting list? Or do you forget to check whether or not God's answered your prayers? Time to catch up with Abraham's servant...

◉ Read Genesis 24 v 15–27

ENGAGE YOUR BRAIN

▷ *Did God answer the servant's prayer?*

▷ *How did he react? (v26–27)*

Abraham sent his servant to find a wife for Isaac. The servant had asked God to lead him to the right family and the right girl. And God did! Nice one — nose rings and bracelets all round (v22). The servant realised God was behind it all and so thanked and praised the Lord for this brilliant answer to prayer.

If you've got time, **read v28–49**. If not, here's what happens:

• Rebekah's brother, Laban, welcomed Abraham's servant into their house.

• The servant told them all about Abraham and how good God had been to him.

• And all about the mission Abraham had sent him on and how God answered his prayer.

◉ Read verses 50–54

▷ *How did Rebekah's brother and father respond to the servant?*

▷ *What did they recognise? (v50)*

God was in complete control. He showed great kindness to Abraham yet again, and answered the servant's prayer. God was looking after His people. Laban and Bethuel saw that God was behind this chain of events, so they let Rebekah leave home.

PRAY ABOUT IT

Make a list of things you've prayed for and how God's answered them. Thank Him for these things. Ask Him to help you notice when He answers your prayers.

THE BOTTOM LINE

God answers prayer. Notice it.

→ TAKE IT FURTHER

For prayer pointers, go to page 116.

45 | Showing promise

God led Abraham's servant to Rebekah and her family. Rebekah is the one God wants Isaac to marry. Time for a tearful farewell...

👁 Read Genesis 24 v 54–60

ENGAGE YOUR BRAIN

▷ *What was the great blessing that Rebekah's family gave her? (v60)*

▷ *How does that fit in with God's plans and promises? (See Genesis 22 v 15–18)*

Rebekah's family wanted her to stay a little longer, but she decided it was time to go and meet the man she would marry. Fair enough.

Rebekah's family hoped she'd have a huge family. Well, she was about to marry Isaac, Abraham's son. God had promised Abraham that His family would be uncountably massive! God was keeping His promise. Abraham and Isaac would have loads of descendants, and they would become God's nation.

Read verses 61–67

▷ *What's the happy ending to this, the longest chapter in Genesis?*

Rebekah and Isaac finally met. They got married and Isaac loved his new wife. Perfect. God had promised to give Isaac a wife, and here she was. God always keeps His promises.

SHARE IT

We've seen throughout Abraham's life, how God keeps His promises and kept giving Abraham far more than he deserved.

▷ *Which of God's promises can you share with your friends?*

▷ *What experiences of God giving you more than you deserve can you share with them?*

PRAY ABOUT IT

It's down to you today...

THE BOTTOM LINE

God keeps ALL His promises.

→TAKE IT FURTHER

Not *take it further* today.

46 End of the road

What would you like to achieve before the end of your life? Abraham had done some great stuff and seen God do incredible things in his long life. But now his time on earth was at an end.

👁 **Read Genesis 25 v 1–6**

ENGAGE YOUR BRAIN
▶ *Why did Isaac get much more than Abraham's other children?*

Isaac was the son God had promised to give Abraham. And it was through Isaac's family that God would keep His most staggering promise.

Find it in **Genesis 12 v 3**.

Isaac got the best inheritance of all. Jesus would be one of his descendants. God would bless people from every nation through Jesus.

👁 **Read Genesis 25 v 7–11**
▶ *What was the final promise to Abraham that God kept? (See Genesis 15 v 15)*

Abraham lived until he was 175. God had been so good to His servant Abraham. And even though Abraham was now dead, God would continue to bless his family. And God's plan

to bless the whole world would continue...

GET ON WITH IT
▶ *What have you learned about God from Abraham's story?*

▶ *What have you learned about Jesus?*

▶ *What have you learned about yourself?*

▶ *What are you going to do about it? What do you need to change?*

PRAY ABOUT IT
Take your time, talking to God about each of your answers.

→ **TAKE IT FURTHER**
Life lessons on page 116.

What's the point?

One of the main ambitions of engage is to encourage you to get stuck into God's word. Each issue, TOOLBOX will give you tips, tools and advice for wrestling with the Bible and understanding it more.

Do you ever read a Bible passage and think *'What is the point of that?'* It's a good question to ask.

WRITING WITH PURPOSE

It sounds obvious when you say it, but the Bible authors wrote their books with a particular purpose in mind. They weren't just scribbling down random things that popped into their heads. We know that, because they often tell us what their aim is.

For instance, near the end of his Gospel, John says: *'Jesus did many other miraculous signs in the presence of his disciples, which are not recorded in this book. But these are written that you may believe that Jesus is the Christ, the Son of God, and that by believing you may have life in his name.'* (John 20 v 30–31)

There are loads of things that John could have told us about Jesus but hasn't. He has selected his material with the specific aim of showing us that Jesus is the Christ, the Son of God, so that we will come to believe in Him and so have eternal life.

Since the writers of the Bible were inspired by God (2 Timothy 3 v 16), their purpose is God's purpose. This means that one of the biggest and most helpful questions we can ever ask is *'Why did the author write this?'*

IT'S OBVIOUS

Sometimes the author bluntly tells us why he is writing his book, in what's sometimes called the *'purpose statement'*. We've already seen one from John's Gospel. Now check out these two: Luke 1 v 1–4
1 John 5 v 13

But what about Bible books that don't obviously state their purpose? Here are a few tips.

1. Get to know the book

Nothing beats reading the whole book several times. Becoming familiar with a Bible book helps you to notice themes running through it and work out the writer's purpose.

2. Ask key questions

These questions are especially helpful if you're reading a New Testament letter (like 1 Timothy) or an Old Testament prophet (like Habakkuk). You might need to grab a study Bible or a commentary to find the answers.

☑ *Who is writing and who's he writing to?*
☑ *What is the situation of the author and the original readers?*
☑ *Are there any problems the author says need to be dealt with?*
☑ *Are there any repeated themes, or a single idea that holds everything together?*

3. What's in and what's out?

'Narrative' books are ones that talk us through historical events (like Genesis or Acts). In these books you can get an idea of the author's purpose from what he chooses to put in and what he leaves out of his account. Sometimes the author hits the accelerator pedal and covers someone's whole life in two verses; at other times he slows down and gives us a few hours in great detail. We should be asking, *'Why do we hear so much about this and so little about that?'*

☑ Read 1 Corinthians 13 on its own and write down the main points you think the passage is making.

☑ Time to play detective. Look up the following verses to get a feel for some of the issues that prompted Paul to write to Christians in Corinth: 1 v 10–12, 3 v 1–4, 4 v 6–10, 6 v 1, 6 v 8, 11 v 17–18.

☑ How do they make you read chapter 13 differently?

In this article we've shown you the very best tool for understanding the Bible. Whenever you read a Bible passage, ask *'What's the author's purpose for writing this?' 'What are the big themes?' ' What is the author trying to do?'* In other words, what's the point?

Ideas taken from Dig Deeper by Nigel Beynon and Andrew Sach (available from www.thegoodbook.com).

47 | Light conversation

Imagine someone wandering around with his eyes firmly shut, bumping into things and saying: 'I refuse to believe the sun's shining'. Of course he can't see the sun, his eyes are shut! If you think that's dumb, meet the Pharisees.

👁 Read John 8 v 12–13

ENGAGE YOUR BRAIN

▶ *What's so amazing about Jesus' huge claim?*

▶ *Did the Pharisees believe Him?*

This is massive. Take it in. Jesus is saying: *'I am the way to God. The only way. Knowing God is all to do with me. Whoever follows me, steps out of the darkness of their sinful ways. They walk with me, serving God and enjoying eternal life.'*

But the Pharisees shut out the light. They refused to believe that Jesus was from God and wouldn't walk His way.

👁 Read verses 14–20

▶ *What two reasons did Jesus give for why they should believe Him?*
▶ *verse 14:*

▶ *verse 18:*

Jesus was clearly from God. It was obvious in everything He did and said. But the Pharisees didn't really know Jesus or His Father. So they wouldn't listen to them.

GET ON WITH IT

▶ *Do you ever try to block out the light from your life?*

▶ *What wrong things in your life has Jesus (the light) shown up?*

▶ *What do you need to do about those things if you follow Jesus?*

PRAY ABOUT IT

Spend time talking to God about your answers.

THE BOTTOM LINE

Jesus is the light — follow Him.

→ TAKE IT FURTHER

Walk into the light on page 116.

48 | Hard truth

The Jewish leaders refused to believe that Jesus was God's Son and that they needed to follow Him. Jesus made sure they knew exactly how serious it was to reject Him.

👁 Read John 8 v 21–24

ENGAGE YOUR BRAIN

▷ *What was Jesus' blunt warning for those who refused to believe He was God's Son? (v24)*

▷ *How does that make you feel?*

It's a horribly painful truth. But it's a truth we have to tackle. People who refuse to believe Jesus, or accept His offer of rescue from their sins, will be punished. They won't be able to live with Jesus. They'll face eternal death.

👁 Read verses 25–30

▷ *Whose words is Jesus speaking? (v26–27)*

▷ *When would they realise who Jesus really was? (v28)*

▷ *Even though the Jewish leaders rejected Him, what was still happening? (v30)*

These men were the nation's masters of religion. Yet they didn't recognise God's words when they heard them.

They'd only realise who Jesus was once they'd lifted Him up to die on the cross... and He'd beaten death by being raised back to life.

GET ON WITH IT

We're living after these events happened, so we have all the evidence in front of us. Do you reject it? Do you accept it? If so, how does it affect the way you live?

PRAY ABOUT IT

Pray for people you know who reject Jesus' message. Talk to God about your own response to Jesus, and your struggles in following Him.

THE BOTTOM LINE

Your turn. Sum up today's Bible bit in one sentence.

→ TAKE IT FURTHER

There isn't one today. Why not spend more time talking to God about your friends who are still walking in darkness?

49 : Finding freedom

What are the signs someone's a Christian? Using clever theological words? Offering to pray for everyone whether they want it or not? Having a really cool-looking Bible? What would you say is the mark of a true Christian?

👁 Read John 8 v 31–32

ENGAGE YOUR BRAIN

▶ *What's the mark of a true disciple of Jesus?*

▶ *What's the promise for those who do that? (v32)*

The test is sticking long-term to Jesus' teaching. Jesus' real disciples carry on living His way, becoming more like Him. By holding to Jesus' teaching, we discover the truth about Jesus and this truth sets us free. But free from what?

👁 Read verses 33–36

▶ *What had these guys failed to grasp? (v33–34)*

▶ *Who needs to be set free? (v34)*

These people were relying on their Jewishness to make them right with God (v33). But Jesus says EVERYONE is a slave to sin and needs to be set free. We've all sinned, no exceptions.

Your background is irrelevant. No one can assume they're automatically in with God. No one can save themselves. Only Jesus can set people free from slavery to sin.

PRAY ABOUT IT

▶ *Has Jesus set you free from sin?*

▶ *Who do you know who needs to be set free?*

▶ *What sin still has its handcuffs on you, keeping you a slave?*

▶ *Do you need help holding on to Jesus' teaching?*

Talk to God about some or all of these things.

THE BOTTOM LINE
Only Jesus sets people free.

➡ TAKE IT FURTHER
Feel free to turn to page 116.

50 Like father, like son

'Ooh, you're just like your dad!' Fed up of hearing embarrassing things like that? Yet there are some people we'd love to be associated with. Who do you most want to be like?

👁 **Read John 8 v 37–43**

ENGAGE YOUR BRAIN

▷ *Who was their hero? (v39)*

▷ *How were they unlike him? (v40)*

▷ *Who else did they claim to be like? (v41)*

▷ *How were they unlike Him? (v42)*

These Jews were really proud of being descended from Abraham, yet they were nothing like him. If they were devoted to God, as Abraham was, they'd believe Jesus' words and follow Him. Instead, they hated His words and wanted to kill Him.

They were also proud of being God's chosen people. But they didn't really love God, or His Son Jesus. They were fakes. So who were they really like?

👁 **Read verses 44–47**

▷ *What was the devastating truth? (v44)*

▷ *Why didn't they understand or believe what Jesus said? (v47)*

These people thought they were OK with God because they were born into the right family. But Jesus dropped a bombshell. Their real father was the devil — he's the one they were most like. The proof was there: they refused to believe Jesus and would soon murder Him.

▷ *Who are your actions, words and thoughts most like?*

▷ *What do you need to change?*

▷ *What do you rely on to make you right with God? Your family, church-going, good deeds? Or do you rely on Jesus' death for you?*

PRAY ABOUT IT

Time to talk to God about this stuff.

→ **TAKE IT FURTHER**

It's child's play on page 117.

51 | I am who I am

Jesus v the Jews. It's getting very tense — Jesus has told them they're the devil's children. They're not too happy about this. Despite being face-to-face with God's Son, they refuse to believe Him.

👁 Read John 8 v 48–52

ENGAGE YOUR BRAIN
- ▶ *How did they insult Jesus?*
- ▶ *How did Jesus defend Himself? (v49–50)*
- ▶ *What incredible claim did He make? (v51)*

This drove the Jews wild with fury. Earlier they'd seemed ready to follow Him (v30); now they wanted to kill Him! They claimed Jesus was demon-possessed. If this was true, He wouldn't be serving God, giving Him the glory (v49). God will judge those who refuse to believe Jesus (v50).

In verse 51, Jesus isn't saying that Christians won't die on earth. He's saying that by trusting in Him, we can be rescued from the punishment of eternal death in hell.

👁 Read verses 53–59
- ▶ *Who **had** believed in Jesus? (v56)*

- ▶ *What astonishing claim did Jesus make? (v58)*

The descendants of Abraham refused to believe Jesus. But Abraham had believed in Jesus. He trusted God's promise to bless all nations through his family. God's promise to Abraham came true in Jesus.

Even more shocking was Jesus' claim to be *'I AM'* — the name God called Himself when speaking to Moses. Jesus claimed to be God! The Jews went ballistic.

PRAY ABOUT IT
- ▶ *Who do you think was right?*
- ▶ *Why?*
- ▶ *So what does that mean for you?*
Talk to God about your answers and anything that's bothering you.

THE BOTTOM LINE
Jesus claimed to be God.

→ TAKE IT FURTHER
Want some more? Dash to page 117.

52 | Seeing the truth

Sit up. Wake up. Listen up.
This next story from Jesus' life is an eye-opener.
Literally.

👁 Read John 9 v 1–5

ENGAGE YOUR BRAIN
▶ *What was the disciples' tricky question?*

▶ *What was Jesus' surprising answer? (v3)*

▶ *What point is Jesus making in verses 4–5?*

Jesus said this man wasn't blind because of any sin in his family. The surprising reason for his blindness was so that people would see God at work in his life.

Jesus was making a far bigger point — He is the light of the world. People desperately need to **see** who Jesus is before the final judgement takes place, and it's too late.

👁 Read verses 6-12
▶ *What eye-opening thing happened?*

▶ *What couldn't the man's neighbours believe? (v8–12)*

His friends couldn't believe it was the same man. But this man trusted Jesus, obeyed Him and His blindness was cured.

If people obey Jesus and trust Him, they can be cured of their sinfulness. But most people refuse to believe. Why do many people find it so hard?

PRAY ABOUT IT
Make a short list below of people you know who are blind about Jesus:

Ask God to use you to point each of them towards the light of Jesus.

→ TAKE IT FURTHER
More truth on page 117.

53 | Blind hate

Ever had an argument with someone, where you've given them all the facts but they simply refuse to see your point of view? The Jewish leaders had seen and heard so much about Jesus, yet still refused to believe.

👁 Read John 9 v 13–17

ENGAGE YOUR BRAIN

▶ *What poor excuse did they have for not believing Jesus? (v16)*

▶ *But what did others say? (v16)*

▶ *Who did the ex-blind man say Jesus was? (v17)*

Jews were forbidden from working on the Sabbath — their holy day. Jesus performed a life-changing miracle and healed a man on the Sabbath. Doesn't sound like work to me.

At least some of the Pharisees asked the right question: *'How could a sinner do such miraculous signs?'* The ex-blind man realised that Jesus had been sent by God, but still hadn't worked out that He was God's Son.

👁 Read verses 18–25

▶ *Why did the man's parents avoid the question? (v22–23)*

▶ *What did the man say this time?*

The Jewish leaders wouldn't accept that Jesus was sent by God. They even threatened to throw people out of the synagogue if they said Jesus was *the Christ* (God's chosen king). That meant they'd be cut off from their friends and become outsiders.

But the ex-blind man stood up to the bullying Pharisees and stuck by the truth (v25).

GET ON WITH IT

▶ *Ever feel under pressure to speak against Jesus?*
▶ *Will you stand up for Him even though it might mean rejection?*

PRAY ABOUT IT

Ask God to give you courage to stand up for Jesus and tell people the truth.

→ TAKE IT FURTHER

For a further grilling, try page 117.

54 | Blinding truth

Imagine a long court case, where day after day of evidence has shown that the defendant must be innocent. But the jury has already decided in advance to convict the man, so he's found guilty. Unbelievable.

👁 Read John 9 v 26–29

ENGAGE YOUR BRAIN

▶ *What did the Pharisees ask the ex-blind man again?*

▶ *What was his brilliant answer?*

▶ *What was their reaction? (v28)*

Great stuff. This man who'd been healed by Jesus was showing how stupid the Pharisees were for refusing to believe the truth about Jesus. He even cheekily asked if they wanted to become Jesus' followers.

They exploded with rage at this, saying they were disciples of Moses, not Jesus. They were making lame excuses for ignoring the signs that pointed to Jesus being God's Son.

👁 Read verses 30–34

▶ *What excellent points did the man make? (v31, 33)*

▶ *How did the Pharisees respond to* *this logical argument? (v34)*

Imagine taking on the religious leaders and showing up their blinkered vision. And all this from a man who'd been blind all his life. But he now saw more than the Pharisees did. He saw that Jesus could do things only God could. So He must be from God. Obvious, really.

PRAY ABOUT IT

If you've still not made your mind up about Jesus, ask God to reveal the truth to you. Keep reading your Bible and weigh up the evidence.

If you're already convinced about Jesus, don't assume you know it all yet. Ask God to show you more about the real Jesus and to challenge you through His teaching.

THE BOTTOM LINE

You have all the evidence.

→ TAKE IT FURTHER

The truth is out there... on page 117.

55 : Blind faith

The story so far: Jesus healed a man who'd been blind since birth. The Pharisees quizzed the man, but refused to believe what Jesus had done. In fact, they threw the ex-blind man out. So Jesus went to find him.

👁 Read John 9 v 35–38

ENGAGE YOUR BRAIN

▶ *What did Jesus ask the man?*

▶ *What was his perfect response? (v38)*

Jesus called Himself the *'Son of Man'* more than any other name. It's a term from the Old Testament, referring to the Messiah who would rule forever (Daniel 7 v 13–14). Jesus was asking this man: *'Do you really believe I'm the King sent by God to rule forever?'*

The ex-blind man was certain of it, and he worshipped Jesus there and then. That's the right way to respond to Jesus — to tell Him that you believe in Him. And to worship Him and serve Him with your whole life.

👁 Read verses 39-41

▶ *Why did Jesus come into the world? (v39)*

▶ *What was the sad truth for the Pharisees? (v41)*

Jesus coming into the world was both a wonderful and terrible event. It resulted in many people being rescued from sin. But those who think they know the truth about God yet reject Jesus, remain guilty before God. And that's very serious.

SHARE IT

▶ *What do these vital truths make you want to say to your friends?*

PRAY ABOUT IT

▶ *What do they make you want to say to Jesus?*

THE BOTTOM LINE

Believe in Jesus and worship Him with your life. Or reject Him and face the consequences.

→ TAKE IT FURTHER

For more on the *'Son of Man'*, try page 118.

56 Feeling sheepish

Jesus has been tangling with the Jewish leaders. They refused to believe He was from God. In return, Jesus said they were serving the devil, not God. Bear all this in mind as you listen in on some 'woolly' teaching.

👁 Read John 10 v 1–6

ENGAGE YOUR BRAIN

▶ *How did Jesus write off the religious leaders? (v1)*

▶ *What did He say about Himself? (v2–4)*

Jesus didn't have many kind words for the Jewish leaders. They were self-appointed, not chosen by God as He was. Because they were serving themselves — not God — they led people away from the Lord.

But Jesus cares deeply for His followers. Unlike the dodgy Pharisees, Jesus knows each of them by name and leads the way, fighting the battles they can't fight and doing the things they can't do.

▶ *What do Jesus' true followers do? (v3)*

▶ *What won't they do? (v5)*

Christians listen to their shepherd, Jesus. They love following Him, living His way. Yes, they may stumble sometimes, but they want to do things His way, pleasing Him.

GET ON WITH IT

It's hard not to listen to other voices — people who lead us away from Jesus.

▶ *Whose words are a bad influence on you?*

▶ *What can you do to make sure you're not led astray?*

PRAY ABOUT IT

Ask God to help you not listen to the wrong voices, but to follow, obey and live only for Jesus.

THE BOTTOM LINE

Follow Jesus. And only Him.

→ TAKE IT FURTHER

Follow the shepherd to page 118.

57 | Gate expectations

Jesus is talking about sheep. Picture the scene: a shepherd's precious flock is kept safe in a pen, protected by a big wall. The only way in is a gate. Sheep make great woolly jumpers but are rubbish wall-jumpers.

👁 Read John 10 v 7–10

ENGAGE YOUR BRAIN

▶ Who is the only way in for the sheep?

▶ What does Jesus call others who claim to be the way to God?

▶ What do they do? (v10)

Jesus is the ONLY way to eternal life. Having a Christian family, living a good life, following the rules — none of it is good enough. We can only get there through Jesus.

Anyone who says otherwise is dangerous. Not just mildly dangerous — they are **thieves and murderers**. Stealing people from the Lord, leading them away from Him to eternal death.

GET ON WITH IT

Know anyone who says you need more than just Jesus to get to heaven? Don't listen to them.

If you're unsure about what someone's saying, check it with the Bible and with older Christians.

▶ What's the fantastic news for those who trust in Jesus? (v9–10)

Whoever turns to Jesus, and trusts in His death for them, will be saved. From sin and death. Forever. Not only that, but Jesus promises them life at its best (v10). And one day, a perfect life with God for all eternity.

PRAY ABOUT IT

You know what to say...

THE BOTTOM LINE

Jesus is the only way to eternal life.

→ TAKE IT FURTHER

One way only... to page 118.

58 | Flock tactics

Ever been surprised by the cost of something? Maybe a present for someone. Or you agreed to help someone out and it took far more time and effort than expected. Jesus knew exactly what it would cost to rescue us...

👁 Read John 10 v 11–15

ENGAGE YOUR BRAIN

Jesus said He came to give us *'life to the full'*.

▶ *What would it cost for Him to give us this life? (v11, 15)*

Jesus wasn't pushed into it. He voluntarily gave up His life for people who needed His rescue. You and me.

👁 Read verses 16–21

▶ *What's Jesus talking about in verse 16?*

▶ *What else would happen to Jesus? (v17–18)*

▶ *What did the Jews think of it all?*

Not only would Jesus give His life to rescue sinners like us, He'd be raised back to life to beat death. And there was more good news...

The Jews thought that only they would go to live with God forever. But Jesus dropped a bombshell — He had come to save non–Jewish people too (v16). They would all be one flock — one big family.

We can see this incredibly diverse family all around us; people from every nation, language and background, all worshipping Jesus.

PRAY ABOUT IT

Thank God for what Jesus has done for you, and what it cost Him.

Pray for Christians you know around the world or from very different backgrounds to yourself.

THE BOTTOM LINE

Jesus laid down His life for His people.

➔ TAKE IT FURTHER

Round the world trip — page 118.

59 | Life-changing words

It's easy to take Jesus' words for granted — especially if you've heard them many times. So, right now, ask God to help you concentrate on Jesus' powerful words today. And be ready for them to have an impact on your life.

👁 Read John 10 v 22–30

ENGAGE YOUR BRAIN

▷ *What was annoying the Jews?*

▷ *What evidence did they already have that Jesus was the Messiah? (v25, 27)*

▷ *What's so sensational about v30?*

▷ *What can people who trust Jesus be sure of?*

v 27:

v 28a:

v 28b:

Jesus refused to say bluntly that He was the Messiah. He wouldn't give the Jewish leaders a further reason to kill Him just yet. Also, most of them were hoping the Messiah would be a freedom–fighter who would lead a rebellion against the Romans.

Jesus' miracles (v25) and words (v27) showed that He was the promised Messiah. But Jesus came to rescue people from *sin*, not the Romans.

The Jews didn't miss verse 30. Jesus said that He and God the Father are so closely related that Jesus' actions are God's actions. Astonishing.

That's awesome news for Christians. They have a close relationship with Jesus; they will live with Him forever; no one can snatch them away from His hands. Mind-blowing stuff.

PRAY ABOUT IT
Read through verses 27–30 again, slowly. Use these verses to help you speak openly with God right now.

→ TAKE IT FURTHER
Want more? Go to page 118.

60 | Stone deaf

In John's Gospel we've seen loads of signs pointing to who Jesus is. We've looked at the evidence of Jesus' words, actions and what others thought of Him. But what do you think about Jesus?

👁 Read John 10 v 31–36

ENGAGE YOUR BRAIN

▷ Why did the crowd want to stone Jesus to death?

▷ Any idea what Jesus is saying in v34–36? Try to sum it up in two sentences.

The Jews couldn't believe that this man Jesus was actually claiming to be God. They wanted to kill Him. So Jesus pointed them to the Scriptures, where God called certain people 'gods' (Psalm 82 v 6). Yet Jesus had been sent by His Father God into the world. Couldn't they see how much more important Jesus was?

👁 Read verses 37–42

▷ What further evidence did Jesus give that He was God's Son? (v37–38)

▷ Who believed Jesus and who didn't? (v39–42)

Jesus was saying: 'If the way I act is any different from the way God acts, don't believe me. But look at all the miracles you've seen. You've got all the evidence you need!'

Jesus blew apart their wrong view of God. Here was God's Son, right in front of them, and yet they still refused to believe.

TALK IT THROUGH

▷ What have you learned about Jesus from John's Gospel?
▷ How does your view of Jesus need to change?
▷ On spare paper, write how you'd describe Jesus and who He is.
▷ So how will that affect the way you live?

PRAY ABOUT IT

Talk to God about all of those things.

→ TAKE IT FURTHER

No take it further today. So why not read John chapters 6–10 again and note what new things you notice?

GOD IS ~~DEAD~~ Dad

In each issue of **engage** we'll take time out to explain a key truth about God, the Bible and Christianity. In ESSENTIAL we'll gather together all the teaching from the Bible on a particular subject, and try to explain it. This issue, we're looking at God the Father.

In the last issue of *engage* we started to look at who God is — and discovered that there's one God in three persons: Father, Son and Spirit. But why is God the Father called *'Father'*? What makes Him a Dad? Why isn't He called an uncle, a brother or just plain Harold, as the kid once said (*'Our Father who art in Heaven, Harold be thy name'*).

The Bible tells us that the three persons of the Trinity are all equally God, but they relate to each other, and the rest of the planet, in different ways.

God the Father is a father in four distinct ways:

1. HE IS JESUS' ETERNAL DAD

Since before the beginning of time,

God the Father and God the Son (Jesus) have related to each other in the same sort of way as a human father and son do. This doesn't mean that God the Father existed before God the Son. But it does mean that their roles and relationship are like those you would see in a perfect family.

God the Father has the authority — He's the one who sends Jesus into the world to do awesome things like saving everyone from their sins (John 3 v 16). He's the one who encourages Jesus and tells Him that He's doing a great job (Mark 1 v 11). He's the one that Jesus turns to when He is at His most scared and the one that Jesus is obedient to (Matthew 26 v 39). And like any father and son, seeing Jesus the Son gives us a glimpse of what the Father is like (John 14 v 9).

2. HE MADE THE WORLD

God the Father spoke the words that created the world (Genesis 1 v 3). He's like the Dad of the planet. And, we, as the pinnacle of His creation, have His *'image'*. Just like all children, we look a bit like the one who gave us life. But although all of us humans are *'God's offspring'* (Acts 17 v 29), sin cuts us off from God the Father — who is the source of our life. In fact, Jesus made it clear that sin actually puts us into a very different kind of family — the devil's (John 8 v 44)!

The story of the Bible is about how this loving creator Father makes it possible for our relationship with Him to be restored.

3. HE CHOSE ISRAEL TO BE HIS CHILDREN

In the Old Testament we learn that God set aside just one nation to have an extra special relationship with Him. He called Israel His *'firstborn'* (Exodus 4 v 22) — the children who would get His special blessing and favour. But that was just a picture of what He was going to do for the whole world through Jesus.

4. HE ADOPTS ALL BELIEVERS

Through trusting in Jesus, we can all receive adoption into God's new family. We can know God, not as a distant Judge, but as the best ever Father, who cares for all our needs. We can pray to Him, calling Him *'Our Father'* (Matthew 6 v 9) — confident that, like any decent dad here on earth, He wants what's best for His children. God the Father will give us just what we need when we need it. (Luke 11 v 9–13).

It's truly amazing that Jesus makes us children of the Dad we always wanted (and some of us never got). He's wise, rich and loves the socks off us. Why not thank Him for that privilege right now...

Haggai

Home truths

Have you seen those maps in the town centre that say 'YOU ARE HERE'? Well, if you're in Haggai then...

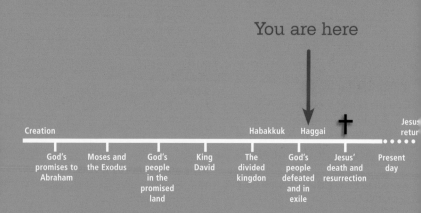

You are here

Creation				Habakkuk	Haggai		Jesus return
God's promises to Abraham	Moses and the Exodus	God's people in the promised land	King David	The divided kingdon	God's people defeated and in exile	Jesus' death and resurrection	Present day

And to be even more exact, the events in this book took place over four months from August 29th to December 18th 520BC, give or take a day... and it was raining (well, OK, not the last part).

God had punished His people for their continuous sin. He let the Babylonians defeat them and carry them off into exile. God's people — well some of them — had finally been set free and come home to Jerusalem. Haggai refers to them as *'the remnant'*, basically the leftovers.

Despite God's goodness in bringing them home, they'd somehow got sidetracked. So instead of re-building God's house, the temple, and living for Him, they'd got busy decorating their own spare rooms.

Enter Haggai with a wake-up call from God, or *'the Lord of Hosts'*, as He's called in Haggai — the commander of all the heavenly armies. God's message to His people was this:

I won't settle for second best!

61 | Home improvement

After the original excitement about re-building God's temple a few years back (find out more in the book of Ezra), things have slowed down. In fact, they've slowed down so much they're not going anywhere.

👁 **Read Haggai 1 v 1–4**

ENGAGE YOUR BRAIN

▶ *What is the people's excuse for not getting on with the job? (v2)*

GET ON WITH IT

'I'll live all out for Jesus once I get to uni — it'll be easier then.'

'I won't get baptised or confirmed just yet. My friends might think I'm weird.'

'I'll take the Bible seriously about not getting drunk after next weekend's party.'

▶ *Is there something you need to stop putting off?*

👁 **Read verses 5–11**

▶ *What has their recent experience been like? (v9–11)*

▶ *What reason does God give for all these frustrations? (v9)*

The panelled houses of v4 are not necessarily particularly fancy, but the point is the people are *busying* themselves with them rather than with God's house (v9). Now you might not be going DIY-crazy in your spare time, but what do you *busy* yourself with? Sport? TV? Fashion? Websites? Something else?

God doesn't live in His temple anymore — we now meet God through Jesus — so how can we put Jesus first in our lives?

PRAY ABOUT IT

Say sorry to God for not putting Him first; ask Him to help you put Jesus first in what you think about, talk about and how you spend your time and money.

THE BOTTOM LINE

'Not yet' isn't good enough for God.

➡ **TAKE IT FURTHER**

For more on Haggai, try page 118.

75

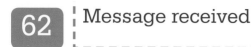

62 | Message received

How often do you see this — God says something and His people actually do it?! Makes a nice change...

👁 Read Haggai 1 v 12–15

ENGAGE YOUR BRAIN

▶ *What's the people's reaction to God's message? (v12)*

▶ *Do you treat God's message in the Bible that way?*

Fearing the Lord doesn't mean becoming a trembling wreck, but it does mean taking Him seriously and recognising that He is in charge.

And despite their wrong priorities in the first half of chapter 1, God speaks to His people, showing them where they're going wrong, and then gives them the massive encouragement of saying He is with them.

PRAY ABOUT IT

If you're a Christian, then God has given you that same promise. One of Jesus' titles is *'Immanuel'*, which means *'God with us'*. Some of Jesus' final words on earth were *'Surely I am with you always, to the very end of*

the age' (Matthew 28 v 20). Why not thank Him for that right now?

▶ *What got the people working hard on the temple? (v14)*

▶ *What does that tell us about the source of any of our good deeds?*

Everything is down to God's grace — the undeserved kindness He shows us. He didn't let the Jews find satisfaction in things that don't last. He let them know where they were going wrong, and He gave them the ability and desire to listen and obey.

SHARE IT

▶ *Can you think of similar examples of God's grace in your life?*
▶ *How can you tell your mates about these experiences?*

THE BOTTOM LINE

God is with His people.

→ TAKE IT FURTHER

Face the fear on page 119.

63 | All shook up

Meanwhile, back at the temple, one month later... the people were fading again. They'd started well and got stuck into rebuilding God's temple. But now, well, was it worth sticking at it?

👁 **Read Haggai 2 v 1–5**

ENGAGE YOUR BRAIN

▶ *How are the older generation feeling? (v3)*

▶ *How does God encourage the people? (v4–5)*

▶ *How long has He had this special relationship (covenant) with His people? (v5 and see timeline)*

Do you ever feel that being a Christian now isn't very impressive. Especially not compared to years ago, when there were masses of people turning to Christ, or believers standing up for Jesus even if it meant a gruesome death?

But God's promises aren't all in the past (like the one He made when He brought His people out of Egypt, v5). He has promises for them now too.

👁 **Read verses 6–9**

▶ *What will God do? (v7)*

▶ *Who does everything belong to?*

The *desired* or *treasure* of all nations referred to in verse 7 is absolutely true — this temple was built using the king of Persia's funds! It also refers to God's kingdom in the future (Hebrews 12 v 26–28) — when God's people from every nation will become a great kingdom that will serve the Lord in glory!

TALK IT THROUGH

Does it sometimes seem as if your church or CU is pretty insignificant? Why not encourage a Christian friend with these verses?

THE BOTTOM LINE

We aren't particularly impressive, but God is.

→ **TAKE IT FURTHER**

For a glimpse of the future, page 119.

64 | Pure and simple

"Ugh! You've got germs — tag!" Ever seen little kids 'passing on' imaginary germs from person to person? Well, the Jews of Haggai's day were seriously infected, and not with imaginary germs, or even a nasty cold...

👁 Read Haggai 2 v 10–14

ENGAGE YOUR BRAIN

▷ *Can holiness be passed on? (v10–12)*

▷ *What about uncleanness? (v13)*

▷ *What point do you think God is making about the people?*

Pretty harsh stuff. Everything the Jews are doing and all the offerings they make in the temple are unclean. Stained by sin. Infected.

👁 Read verses 15-19

▷ *What did God want from His people? (v17)*

God's blessing is not dependent on outward actions like building a temple, going to church or youth group, or using *engage*. God wants our hearts, but we're still infected by sin and we need an antidote.

▷ *Amazingly, what is God's promise to His people (v19)?*

The temple was not only a sign of God living among His people; it was a place where God made it possible for perfect holiness to live with sinful people. The sacrifices carried out by the priests were a way of getting rid of sin, for a short while, at least.

▷ *How does Jesus solve this problem for good?*

PRAY ABOUT IT

Have you grasped the fact that every part of your life has been infected by sin? Spend some time talking to God about that. And thank Him for sending the cure — Jesus.

THE BOTTOM LINE

We are infected by sin. Jesus provides the antidote.

→ TAKE IT FURTHER

For more on the cure, page 119.

Lord of the ring

Date: December 18th 520BC. Let's take a peek at God's final message via Haggai — marked PRIVATE for Zerubbabel, the governor of Judah — but very important for us too.

👁 **Read Haggai 2 v 20–23**

ENGAGE YOUR BRAIN

▷ *Have we seen this earth-shaking language before in Haggai?*

▷ *What is God going to do next time He shakes the earth (v22)?*

Evil always contains the seeds of its own destruction (see the end of v22). How many world leaders can you think of who have been caught out by their double standards and dodgy dealings? God is far more powerful than the military or media.

▷ *Who was Zerubbabel?*

OK, so you might not have heard of him. He was the grandson of the last ever king of Judah. He was also a descendant of King David, who God promised would always have a descendent on his throne.

But Zerubbabel wasn't a king — just the local governor. In fact, God had said to Zerubbabel's grandfather, Jehoiachin: *'If you... were a signet ring* (a seal of royal authority) *on my right hand, I would still pull you off. I will hand you over to those who seek your life.'* (Jeremiah 22 v 24-25)

▷ *So, how does God reassure Zerubbabel (v23)?*

This is an awesome promise that God makes to Zerubbabel. But Zerubbabel never got to be king. Did God's promise fail? Check out **Matthew 1 v 12–16**. Zeb was an ancestor of King Jesus who will rule forever.

PRAY ABOUT IT
Thank God for specific stuff He has taught you through the book of Haggai. And thank Him for Jesus, the everlasting King.

THE BOTTOM LINE
God's King, Jesus, will rule forever.

➡ **TAKE IT FURTHER**
For the final word on Haggai — p119.

Cash values

Have you ever day-dreamed about winning a huge pile of money? What would you spend it on? A round-the-world plane ticket? Fast car? Designer-clothes shopping spree? Or would you give it all away to the *Twilight Home for Aged Donkeys*?

Back to reality. Maybe you have an allowance or a part time or full time job. What do you spend your money on? Music? High street shopping sprees? Or do you sponsor Jemima for £2 a week down at the donkey sanctuary? Whether you've got a lot or a little, the Bible has a lot to say about money.

DANGER MONEY

First of all, it's dangerous. 1 Timothy 6 v 10 tells us *'the love of money is the root of all kinds of evil'*. Sounds pretty harsh? How can a few metal coins or banknotes be evil? It's not money itself that is so bad — it's *loving* it. We were created to love God, to live in a relationship with Him. More than that, if we're Christians, we were

ransomed — bought by Christ's death to belong to Him forever. So why are we having a sordid affair with money and all it can buy us?

A quick look at 1 Timothy chapter 6 spells out the danger of loving money — it can lead to loss of faith and ultimately destruction (v9-10). Why? It makes us arrogant and stops us trusting God (v17).

Imagine for a moment that you've got it all: private jet, holiday homes all over the world, numerous fast cars — whatever you want it's yours. Are you going to realise that you're actually a rotten sinner who needs God? Or will you be arrogant? And where will you find your security? In your bodyguard, bulletproof car, trust fund, investment portfolio and multi-million-dollar insurance policies? Or in God?

GIVE IT UP?

So what do we do? Sell everything and go live in a tent? Sponsor Betty *and* Jemima? God's not a killjoy. He created everything for our enjoyment, but remember that it all belongs to Him in the first place. Chances are if you're reading this that you've got far more material wealth than 90% of the world, so *'be generous and willing to share'* (1 Tim 6 v 18).

Why? Well look at who we're following: *'For you know the grace of our Lord Jesus Christ, that though he was rich, yet for your sakes he became poor, so that you through his poverty might become rich'* (2 Corinthians 8 v 9).

And it shouldn't be a miserable duty — *'God loves a cheerful giver'* (2 Corinthians 9 v 7).

But before you rush off to double your donation to the *Twilight Home for Aged Donkeys*, think for a second. Lots of people support cancer charities, flood victims and donkey sanctuaries. Give money to them by all means, but if you're a Christian, what matters most to you? Why not focus on organisations who share the good news of Jesus with people, or who translate the Bible into new languages, or who look after Christians who are tortured and lose everything they have for following Jesus. If we don't support them, who will?

SAFE INVESTMENT

What we do with money says a lot about who we are and what really matters to us. Jesus sums it up in Matthew 6 v 19-21: *'Do not store up for yourselves treasures on earth, where moth and rust destroy, and where thieves break in and steal. But store up for yourselves treasures in heaven, where moth and rust do not destroy, and where thieves do not break in and steal. For where your treasure is, there your heart will be also.'*

Where is your heart? On the High Street or in the Highest?

1 Timothy

Holy housework

Hi Tim!
Having a fantastic time on our
hols. Place is lovely. Dad's got
sunburn — already! Sorry, forgot
to stock up on cat food before we
left. Can you get some? (Sardine
& trout's her favourite) Oh, and
make sure you tidy up the house
before we get back. Right, I'm off
to the pool...
Love, Mum x x x

Oh brilliant. They get a suntan while
you're grovelling under the sofa,
hoovering up cat hairs.

You're getting the flavour of Paul's
first letter to Timothy, a young-ish
Christian leader who's in charge of a
church that has problems. Paul's not
writing to tell Tim about his suntan.
He's got more urgent matters in
mind, which will involve some pretty
tough work for Tim.

Here's how Paul put it:
*'Although I hope to come to
you soon, I am writing you*
*these instructions so that, if
I am delayed, you will know
how people ought to conduct
themselves in God's household...'*
(1 Timothy 3 v 14–15)

Paul's got a job for Timothy to do
— to sort the house out. Or, to be
precise, to sort God's household out.
To get the church in order. To get its
members behaving and relating to
each other as God wanted.

Like vacuuming out the cat hairs,
it would be a painfully testing job.
Tim would have to confront people,
challenge them, sometimes tell them
off. He'd make enemies. Paul told
Timothy it would be like a fight. But it
had to be done because the church is
God's household — it must live in line
with God's truth.

**Christians are all part of God's
family, the church. So Paul's words
matter to us too. Get ready for
some spring-cleaning...**

82

66 | False start

Ever talked with someone from a cult? They quote from the Bible and seem to know it better than we do. But it's dangerous: they pick bits from the Bible, and use them wrongly. It's not a new problem; Paul had it in his day too.

👁 Read 1 Timothy 1 v 1–2

ENGAGE YOUR BRAIN

▷ Who appointed Paul to his role as an apostle?

▷ How did he describe his relationship with Timothy?

Paul was an *apostle* — someone sent out by God to teach people about Jesus. In his letter to Timothy, Paul makes it clear that he's the boss. It's packed full of fatherly advice, commands and encouragement.

👁 Read verses 3–7

▷ What did Paul tell Tim to do? (v3)

▷ What did Paul think of these dodgy teachers? (v6–7)

It was vital that Timothy stuck with this church and stood against the false teachers. Their teaching was based on myths and family trees (genealogies), not on Jesus and God's word. It led to controversy, not faith.

▷ What does true, godly teaching lead to?

This false teaching was preventing love in the church — love for God and love for each other. Paul said that love comes from:

– **a pure heart** (made clean by Jesus)
– **a good conscience** (obeying God, avoiding sin)
– **a sincere faith** (not just on Sundays).

PRAY ABOUT IT

Ask God to help you stand up to people whose teaching isn't based on God's word and doesn't promote love. Ask Him to help you develop a pure heart, a good conscience, and sincere faith in Jesus.

THE BOTTOM LINE

Truthful teaching leads to love.

→ TAKE IT FURTHER

More from Paul on page 119.

Point of law

How many of the 10 Commandments can you name off the top of your head? (Jot them down, then check in Exodus 20 v 1–17.) What's the point of Old Testament law, such as the 10 Commandments?

👁 Read 1 Timothy 1 v 8–11

ENGAGE YOUR BRAIN

▶ *What does Paul say about the Old Testament ('the law')? (v8)*

▶ *Who is the law really for? (v9–10)*

▶ *So what's the point of Old Testament law?*

The Old Testament isn't there to merely give us brilliant, exciting and gory stories. It's not there for self-righteous teachers like the ones Paul's been warning us against (v7). It is for sinners — ordinary people like us. God's law is God's perfect standard for living, and it shows up our sinfulness. It makes us realise we need to change our ways.

▶ *What's the test for right teaching? (v10–11)*

The Old T shows us God's perfect standards and leads us to the gospel — what God has done for us through Jesus (v11). We can't meet God's sinless standard by ourselves. Only Jesus dying in our place can make us right with God.

GET ON WITH IT

How can you make sure you read and know more of the Old Testament? Maybe you coud ask a leader at church to find you a plan for reading through the whole Bible. Or make yourself one. Or go to *Take it further*.

PRAY ABOUT IT

Read the 10 Commandments in **Exodus 20 v 1–17**. Talk to God about the sins you really struggle with.

THE BOTTOM LINE

Hold on to the Old Testament — it points us to Jesus.

→ TAKE IT FURTHER

Want to read the whole OT? Check out page 120.

68 | Amazing grace

Are you excited about the gospel — the truth of what God has done through Jesus? Try to talk about the gospel, non-stop, for a minute. Go on. Paul was massively excited about Jesus Christ...

👁 Read 1 Timothy 1 v 12–14

ENGAGE YOUR BRAIN
▶ *How would you describe Paul's life before he came to know Jesus? (v13)*

▶ *What did he recognise had happened to him? (v14)*

Paul was thrilled to talk about Jesus and what He'd done. Paul knew he'd been a nasty piece of work — hunting down and persecuting Christians. But He'd seen God transform his life, through the faith and love of Jesus.

👁 Read verses 15–17
▶ *Why did Jesus come into the world? (v15)*

▶ *Why did God choose to save someone as evil as Paul? (v16)*

Amazing stuff. Jesus Christ, God's own Son, became human to save disgusting sinners like us! He even forgave an enemy of God like Paul. By doing this, God showed how incredibly gracious, patient and forgiving He is. If Paul can be changed by God, anyone can. Yes, ANYONE. They just have to believe in Jesus and receive eternal life (v16).

PRAY ABOUT IT
Pray for people you can barely imagine becoming Christians. Ask for Jesus to transform their lives through His grace, love and forgiveness. Then use verse 17 to give God the praise He deserves.

THE BOTTOM LINE
Christ Jesus came into the world to save sinners.

→ TAKE IT FURTHER
For Paul's backstory, go to page 121.

85

69 Fighting talk

Yesterday, Paul distracted himself a little, getting all excited about the gospel and the amazing way Jesus had changed his life. But now he's back to telling Tim what the deal is.

👁 Read 1 Timothy 1 v 18–20

ENGAGE YOUR BRAIN

▶ What did Timothy have to live up to? (v18)

▶ How did Paul describe Timothy's difficult task? (end of v18)

We don't know what the *'prophecies'* about Timothy were. But we know that there was expectation on his shoulders. People expected him to serve God and fight against God's enemies — especially false teachers who led people away from Jesus.

▶ What must Tim do? (v19a)

▶ What happens if we let go of our faith and our obedience to God? (v19b)

Paul urged Tim to hold on to his faith and to keep a good conscience by living in a way that pleased God. To let go of these two things would be disastrous for his faith.

It was vital that Timothy stuck to his task, and it's vital that Christians today do the same. It's difficult in a world full of so many distractions and temptations. But we're in a battle, and we need to make sure we're fighting for the right side. God's side.

PRAY ABOUT IT

1. Pray for Christian friends — that they'll keep on fighting, holding on to their faith, and living God's way.
2. Pray for anyone you know whose faith has been shipwrecked.

THE BOTTOM LINE

Fight the good fight.

→ TAKE IT FURTHER

What's v20 talking about? Find out on page 121.

70 Pray for everyone

In Timothy's church, it seems people were teaching the lie that the gospel — the truth of God's great rescue — was only for certain people. Paul was going to blow that theory out of the water.

👁 Read 1 Timothy 2 v 1–2

ENGAGE YOUR BRAIN

▷ *What does Paul urge Timothy to pray? (v2)*

▷ *Who should he pray this for?*

Paul says *'pray for everyone'*. Bring variety into your prayers — pray for specific needs, pray for general problems, pray with thanksgiving. Pray for all kinds of people — everyone needs to be saved by Jesus.

PRAY ABOUT IT

Paul also encourages us to pray for *'all those in authority.'* Take time out to make a prayer list of people in authority. Try to pray for at least one of these people/groups every day.

👁 Read verses 3–8

▷ *Why should we pray for everyone that they'll come to know Jesus? (v3–4)*

Paul gives us stacks of reasons to pray for people:

1. It pleases God that we pray (v3).
2. He wants *everyone* to be saved (v4)
3. There's only one God (v5); people need to know this.
4. There's only one way to God — through Jesus (v5).
5. Jesus died on *everyone's* behalf(v5)
6. Paul preached to Gentiles (non-Jews) as well as Jews. The gospel is for *everyone*.

GET ON WITH IT

The great news of Jesus is for everyone, so tell them. And get praying for them — for friends, family, enemies, teachers, presidents, plumbers — everyone. Make a list, and start praying right now. Use verses 1–2 to help you.

THE BOTTOM LINE

Pray for everyone — they all need Jesus.

→ TAKE IT FURTHER

Turn to page 121 for more on v8.

71 | Controversial stuff

Do you enjoy controversy or avoid it at all costs? Are you more likely to get on your high horse with your opinions or dive under a table to dodge an argument? Paul has something controversial to say. Especially if you're female.

👁 Read 1 Timothy 2 v 9–10

ENGAGE YOUR BRAIN
- ▶ *What are Paul's fashion tips?*
- ▶ *In what ways should women aim to be attractive? (v10)*

Clearly some women in Timothy's church were more interested in dressing extravagantly and getting noticed for their appearance than for living God-pleasing lives. Paul says *'Dress in a way that's attractive... to God.'* Live attractive lives, rather than trying to impress others with your appearance.

👁 Read verses 11–15

- ▶ *What is not a woman's role in church, according to Paul? (v12)*
- ▶ *What reasons does he give? (v13)*

These women wouldn't accept the teaching of the church's leaders and pushed themselves forward. Paul says it's not right for women to teach men in church. It would reverse God's created order (v13). Paul isn't saying

women have no contribution to make in church — He's saying that men and women should stick to their God-given roles.

It's not all negative! Paul says *'A woman should learn.'* This was controversial too, as many Jewish leaders wouldn't let women be taught from God's word at all. (For more on this whole issue try page 121.)

TALK IT THROUGH
- ▶ *How does today's teaching make you feel? Why?*
Write down any questions you have and ask an older Christian.

THE BOTTOM LINE
Ask God to help you understand anything that has angered or confused you. Ask Him to help you trust Him and obey His word.

→ TAKE IT FURTHER
Controversy continues on page 121.

72 | Leading example

What do you look for in church leaders?
What do you expect them to be like?
What do you expect them not to do?
Circle the ideas below that match your own.

Church leaders should be:

godly   guitar-playing   cool
single   married   male   female
bearded   middle-aged   under 30
wear suits   preachers   Christian
kind   have kids   organised
know the Bible   hospitable

Church leaders should NOT be:

under 30   ugly   rude
new Christians   old Christians
male   female   cool   untrained
out of touch   argumentative
Welsh   lacking in Bible knowledge

👁 Read 1 Timothy 3 v 1–7

ENGAGE YOUR BRAIN

ⅅ *How does Paul describe the job of a church leader? (v1)*

ⅅ *What must leaders be like? (v2–7)*

ⅅ *Why do they need a good reputation outside the church?*

In the New Testament, church leaders are called *'overseers'* or *'elders'* or

'pastors'. Different names, same job. Paul was pretty clear on what they should be like: responsible, respectable, self-controlled, hospitable, good teachers, with a good reputation. Not violent, argumentative, hard-drinking, money-chasing, proud or brand new Christians.

That's a long list. No wonder Paul says that anyone who sets their heart on church leadership *'desires a noble task.'* These guys deserve our respect and support.

PRAY ABOUT IT

Pray for your church and youth leaders. Ask God to help them keep going and help them with the things they really struggle with.

→ TAKE IT FURTHER

A few more prayer hints on page121.

73 Serving suggestions

Timothy's church had a problem with false teachers. So Paul's been telling Tim what to look for in his leaders. Now he turns to deacons — others who serve in the church.

👁 Read 1 Timothy 3 v 8–13

ENGAGE YOUR BRAIN

▶ What must those who serve in church do? (v9)

▶ What are the great benefits of serving the church? (v13)

It's important that those who serve Jesus in their church live a godly life. They must be people who deserve respect, not heavy-drinkers or self-promoters. OK, they will mess up sometimes, but they must strive to live lives that please God.

GET ON WITH IT

▶ How will you serve in your church?

▶ Is there anything you need to change in your life, so you can serve God even better?

👁 Read verses 14–16

▶ Why did Paul write all these instructions?

▶ How does he describe the church? (v15)

▶ How does he describe Jesus?(v16)

The church (all Christians) are *'God's household'* — God's family. They are the *'foundation of the truth.'* Did you realise you were part of something so amazing and important? The church holds on to and spreads the great truth about Jesus (v16).

PRAY ABOUT IT

Ask God to help you get involved in serving the church — other Christians. Ask Him to help you with anything that's getting in the way of you serving Him well.

→ **TAKE IT FURTHER**

More about Jesus on page 122.

74 | Don't eat that, don't marry him

Heard any weird ideas about what it means to be a true Christian? Anyone told you that you need to do (or stop doing) certain things to be accepted by God? Paul stomps on such wrong teaching...

👁 Read 1 Timothy 4 v 1–2

ENGAGE YOUR BRAIN

▷ How does Paul describe false teachers? (v2)

▷ Where does such misleading teaching really come from? (v1b)

These guys were calling themselves Christians but were teaching seriously wrong views that were leading people away from Jesus, eventually abandoning their faith. Such false teaching and lies are evil and must be stamped out, says Paul.

👁 Read verses 3–5

▷ What were they teaching?

▷ What can you think of today that's like this teaching?

▷ How does Paul answer this negative teaching? (v4–5)

By saying *'Don't get married'* or *'Don't eat this'*, these guys were saying *'You get saved by what you do and don't do.'* Complete rubbish.

Only faith in Christ can make us right with God. If anyone says you have to do this or not do that to be a Christian, they're lying. Yes, we want to do what's right and live God's way, but that's a sign of gratitude and obedience to God. It doesn't save us. Only Jesus can do that.

PRAY ABOUT IT

Spend time praising God for some of the great things He's created (including tasty nosh and marriage!). Ask Him to help you not be misled by wrong teaching.

THE BOTTOM LINE

It's not down to what you do or don't do. It's all down to Jesus.

→ TAKE IT FURTHER

Don't do that; go to page 122.

75 Body building

Timothy had to deal with false teachers in his church. A tough task. Like all of us who are trying to serve God, Timothy needed encouragement and a shove in the right direction.

👁 Read 1 Timothy 4 v 6–10

ENGAGE YOUR BRAIN

▶ How does Paul describe the wrong teaching? (v7)

▶ Why should Tim drive out these false teachers? (v6)

▶ Why is godly living even better than a good body? (v8)

Superb encouragement and advice from Paul: If you want to be a good minister, Timothy, carry on teaching the truth. Have nothing to do with teaching that doesn't come from God's word — it's all old wives' tales.

Instead, train yourself to be godly. It will have a huge impact on your life, and unlike physical fitness, the benefits will last for eternity.

We have to work at it. It will be a struggle (v10a). But it's not all down to us — it's down to God, who saves those who put their hope in Him.

GET ON WITH IT

▶ How hard are you working at living a godly life?

Devise a **training routine** to help you grow. Set times when you'll read the Bible, pray, help out at church, meet with other Christians to read the Bible and pray together.

PRAY ABOUT IT

Have you planned your training routine yet? Do it now. And then talk to God about it, asking Him to help you stick at it.

THE BOTTOM LINE

Train yourself to be godly.

→ TAKE IT FURTHER

Pump it up on page 122.

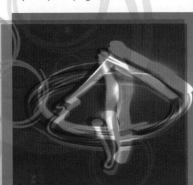

76 Too much too young?

Ever been looked down on by older Christians because you're young? Ever felt you're a bit too young to make a real impact as a Christian? Paul has some wise words for you:

👁 **Read 1 Timothy 4 v 11–12**

ENGAGE YOUR BRAIN

▶ *Should somebody's age get in the way of spreading the gospel?*

▶ *In which areas should you set an example for other believers?*

When we're young, we can sometimes be uneven in our faith — concentrating on certain parts of our Christian lives, but neglecting others. Paul says *'Sort your whole life out, so that you're an example to others.'* Then your age won't be an issue.

GET ON WITH IT

▶ *Speech – how do you need to change the way you talk?*

▶ *Life – how could the way you live be a better example of godly living?*

▶ *Love – Do you show your care for others (not just close friends) in practical ways?*

▶ **Faith** — What do you need to trust God about? That you're saved? That He's with you? That He hears your prayers?

▶ **Purity** — What parts of your life are not pure? What will you do about it?

👁 **Read verses 13–16**

Paul's advice is for church leaders. But verse 16 applies to all of us. *'Watch your life and your doctrine'* (your beliefs). We need to keep checking that we're living lives that please God. And we need to make sure that our beliefs are in line with God's word.

PRAY ABOUT IT

Look back at *GET ON WITH IT*. Talk through your answers with God.

THE BOTTOM LINE

Set an example in speech, life, love, faith and purity.

➡ **TAKE IT FURTHER**

You're not too young to go to p.122.

77 Family fortunes

Do you get on well with older Christians?
How do you treat people younger than you ?
What about the way you are with the opposite sex?

👁 Read 1 Timothy 5 v 1–2

ENGAGE YOUR BRAIN

▶ *How should you not treat older Christians?*

▶ *What should your relationship with older Christians be like?*

When you're young it's easy to tell people exactly what you think of them, or be a bit cheeky. Paul says *'Show older Christians proper respect.'* Show them the same respect, politeness and love you should show your parents. If you think they've done wrong, don't tell them off in a disrespectful way.

▶ *How do your attitudes towards older Christians need to change?*

👁 Read verses 1–2 again

▶ *How should you treat younger Christians?*

▶ *What about members of the opposite sex? (v2)*

The church is a family. That means close relationships. It also means treating people with respect, as equals. It means not patronising, bullying or embarrassing younger kids. It means remembering that Christians of the opposite sex are your brothers and sisters in Christ, not eye-candy. Treat them with respect, and act towards them in a way that's pure and pleases God.

GET ON WITH IT

▶ *Which younger people do you need to treat better?*
▶ *How could your attitude towards the opposite sex be more godly?*

PRAY ABOUT IT

Talk with God about any issues raised today.

THE BOTTOM LINE

Check the way you relate to Christians of all ages.

➔ TAKE IT FURTHER

Follow the family line to page 123.

78 | Widow of opportunity

Life as a church leader is tough — so many problems to deal with, people to look after and to teach. Paul has some more advice for Timothy and his church in Ephesus.

👁 **Read 1 Timothy 5 v 3–8**

ENGAGE YOUR BRAIN

▶ *Who should look after elderly Christians? (v4)*

▶ *Why? (end of v4)*

▶ *What does Paul say to people who don't look after their families? (v8)*

Yesterday Paul taught us to have respect for members of our church family, the church. But we should also look after the people who cared for us and brought us up (v4). Especially elderly relatives who can't care for themselves.

GET ON WITH IT

▶ *Is there anyone in your family you can show more care to?*

▶ *Can you encourage other members of your family to look after elderly relatives?*

ENGAGE YOUR BRAIN

▶ *Who should the church care for? (v5)*

It's the church's responsibility to look after widows who are left alone with no family. Especially the ones who put their hope in God and not in pleasure-seeking (v5–6).

GET ON WITH IT

▶ *Is there anyone elderly and alone at your church you could help?*

▶ *What will you do for them?*

PRAY ABOUT IT

Pray for people you know who are in need. Ask God to help you show more love and care to those left lonely and in need.

THE BOTTOM LINE

Look after the lonely.

→ **TAKE IT FURTHER**

A tiny bit more on page 123.

79 | Merry widows

Any idea what a 'widows list' is? No, me neither. We're not sure exactly what the list is that Paul's talking about. But that doesn't matter — there's still loads from Paul's teaching that we can apply to our lives.

👁 Read 1 Timothy 5 v 9–16

ENGAGE YOUR BRAIN

▶ *What did a widow need to do to qualify for the list?*

Whatever the list was, it's clear that if you were on it, the church would look after you. Only widows over 60 need apply. This group of older women served God and the church in a special way. They showed hospitality, washed other Christians' disgusting, dusty feet, and helped out those in trouble, as well as doing tons of good deeds.

We can often dismiss elderly widows as not much use. Or ignore them completely. But they can do so much to serve God and His people.

GET ON WITH IT

▶ *Which elderly ladies in your church can you talk to more and get to know?*

Write their names down and try to pray for them every week.

👁 Read verses 11–16

▶ *What things got in the way of these women serving Jesus?*

It seems that some of the younger widows had pledged themselves to the Lord's work and not to marry. But then other things — falling in love, gossiping — got in the way of their commitment to Jesus.

PRAY ABOUT IT

▶ *What things get in the way of you serving Jesus?*

Pray about these things, asking God to help you throw out stuff that stops you being committed to Him.

→ TAKE IT FURTHER

For further assistance, try page 123.

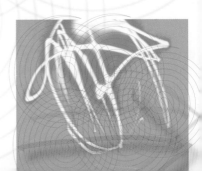

80 | Double honour

What do you think of your church and youth leaders?
What good things do they do?
Do they get the respect and thanks they deserve?

👁 Read 1 Timothy 5 v 17–25

ENGAGE YOUR BRAIN

▶ *What do good leaders deserve? (v17)*

▶ *What should we do if we hear worrying rumours about our leaders? (v19)*

Paul gave Tim advice on appointing leaders (v22) and disciplining them when they did wrong (v20–21). But since you're probably not in charge of a church, let's focus in on verses 19–21 and our attitudes towards our Christian leaders.

1. HONOUR THOSE IN AUTHORITY

Church leaders have a tough job. Responsibility isn't easy. These guys are serving God and deserve respect.

2. HONOUR THOSE WHO TEACH US

It's a huge privilege to learn from God's word. The Lord speaks to us through preachers and youth leaders.

They put loads of time into studying, understanding and teaching the Bible.

▶ *Do you ever thank them or talk to them about their talks?*

3. PAY LEADERS FAIRLY

This seems obvious. Yet many Christian workers are paid poorly, overworked and given little respect or thanks.

▶ *Is there anything you could do for a Christian worker you know who feels unappreciated?*

4. DON'T LISTEN TO RUMOURS

Christian leaders are always under attack. We sometimes don't realise all the hurtful things that are said to them or about them. Don't spread rumours and don't listen to rumours.

PRAY ABOUT IT

Spend five minutes praying for your church and youth leaders.

→ TAKE IT FURTHER

Follow the leader... to page 123.

Work it out

Ever feel like a slave? Either in a job, at school or at home? How would you sum up your attitude towards your 'boss' or 'slave master'?

👁 **Read 1 Timothy 6 v 1–2**

ENGAGE YOUR BRAIN

▶ *What does Paul say our attitude towards our boss (or teacher or parent) should be? (v1)*

▶ *Why? (v1)*

We may not like it, but we've got to show respect to those who have authority over us. That means doing what they say, not talking back or making life difficult for them. Why? Because non–Christians notice the way Christians act. Showing disrespect to bosses, parents or teachers reflects badly on God — our ultimate boss.

▶ *Should we expect Christian bosses to be softer on us? (v2)*

▶ *What should be our attitude towards our Christian boss?*

▶ *Why? (v2)*

We can sometimes expect an easy ride from other Christians. Paul says *'Work even harder for Christians!'* It's an opportunity to serve your Christian brother or sister. You're both working for God. So don't slack off.

GET ON WITH IT

▶ *How does your attitude to your 'boss' and work need to change?*

▶ *How can you show them greater respect?*

▶ *How can you serve another Christian this week?*

PRAY ABOUT IT

What has challenged you today? Talk it over with God and ask Him to help you change the way you work.

THE BOTTOM LINE

Show respect to your boss.

➡ **TAKE IT FURTHER**

Work your way towards page 123.

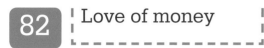

82 | Love of money

Do you think it's better to be rich or poor?
What's your attitude to money?
Would you like more?
Why/why not?

👁 Read 1 Timothy 6 v 3–5

ENGAGE YOUR BRAIN

▷ *What were these men wrongly teaching? (end of v5)*

▷ *What five things did their teaching result in? (v4–5)*

Leaders in Tim's church were greedily flattering and exploiting wealthy church members. The were not teaching the truth about Jesus. Paul said these men were robbing people of the truth. Teaching that godliness leads to wealth is nonsense. It results in envy, bitterness and arguments.

👁 Read verses 6–10

▷ *What's really worth having? (v6,8)*

▷ *Why? (v7)*

▷ *What are the dangers of wanting to be rich? (v9–10)*

Whether we're wealthy or poor, we always want more. But God has already given us so much, and we should be content with that. We haven't earned the things we have — they're all given to us by God.

Love of money is the devil's trap. Once you start chasing money and possessions, you're never satisfied. You always want more cash, nicer clothes, better gadgets. It also leads to many other temptations and sins (v10) and even to wandering away from faith in Jesus. Read verses 9-10 again, taking them very very seriously.

PRAY ABOUT IT

▷ *What have you been challenged about today?*
▷ *What will you do about it?*
           Tell God about it right now.

THE BOTTOM LINE

'Love of money is a root of all kinds of evil.'

➡ TAKE IT FURTHER

More about money on page 123. And check out *Stuff* on page 80.

83 | Fighting talk

What advice would you give to someone who wanted to be a man or woman of God? What should they aim for? Compare your ideas with Paul's...

👁 Read 1 Timothy 6 v 11–12

ENGAGE YOUR BRAIN

▷ *What should the man/woman of God chase after? (v11)*

▷ *What does it mean to 'fight the good fight of faith'?*

Flee from the love of money. It can pull you away from God.

Pursue right-living, godliness, faith, love, gentleness and sticking at it.

Fight the good fight of the faith. Keep going. Give your everything to living for God.

Take hold of eternal life. God has rescued you from sin. Live like someone who'll live forever with God.

👁 Read verses 13–16

Is that the longest sentence you've ever read? Here's how *The Message* phrases it:

'I'm charging you before the life-giving God and before Christ, who took his stand before Pontius Pilate and didn't give an inch: Keep this command to the letter, and don't slack off. Our Master, Jesus Christ, is on his way. He'll show up right on time, his arrival guaranteed by the Blessed and Undisputed Ruler, High King, High God. He's the only one death can't touch, his light so bright no one can get close. He's never been seen by human eyes — human eyes can't take him in! Honour to him, and eternal rule! Oh yes.'

Paul encourages Tim to stick at it — He's serving an awesome God.

PRAY ABOUT IT

Look back at **flee, pursue, fight, take hold**. Talk to God about how you're doing with these four things. Ask Him to help you with the ones you struggle with.

→ TAKE IT FURTHER

More help on sticking at it: page 124.

84 | Real riches

Money was a big issue for Tim's church. Those with no money wanted to get rich quick but ended up giving in to temptation and sin. But the people who were well-off had problems too.

👁 Read 1 Timothy 6 v 17–19

ENGAGE YOUR BRAIN

▶ *What mistakes were rich people in the church making? (v17)*

▶ *Where should they put their trust and hope?*

People who have a comfortable life (that includes most of us) can become arrogant. They trust in their own abilities and their money to get them through life. Paul says *'Don't be so dumb — you can't put your trust in such uncertain things. Take your eyes off them and focus on trusting in and living for God. Then you'll really enjoy all He's given you.'*

▶ *What positive things should we be doing? (v18)*

▶ *Why? What's at stake? (v19)*

If God has given you stuff, be generous and give to others. Share what you have. Do good things for others. Enjoy what God has given you and share it with people.

We shouldn't be looking to grab what we can in this life. We must serve God with what we've got, be generous, and enjoy the rewards and perfect life of eternity with God.

GET ON WITH IT

▶ *Who will you give to and what can you give to them?*
▶ *Who can you do good deeds for?*

PRAY ABOUT IT

Ask God to help you actually do these things. Ask Him to help you fix your sights on serving Him and eternity with Him, not on getting what you can right now.

THE BOTTOM LINE

Give generously and trust in God.

→ TAKE IT FURTHER

More money matters on page 124.

85 | Final words

Paul has reached the end of his long letter to Timothy. In it he has encouraged Tim to stand up to false teaching and to stick at right living. Take it away Paul, one last time...

👁 Read 1 Timothy 6 v 20–21

ENGAGE YOUR BRAIN

▷ *Any ideas what Timothy had to guard?*

Paul was telling Tim to hold on to the truth of the gospel. To keep teaching people the truth about Jesus, especially as others were teaching lies. It's vital for Christians to know what they believe, to hold on to that truth and to share it with others.

GET ON WITH IT

▷ *How can you learn more of God's great truth and understand the gospel better?*

▷ *Who can you talk to about Jesus?*

ENGAGE YOUR BRAIN

▷ *What two things must Tim turn away from? (v20)*

▷ *What's the danger if he doesn't? (v21)*

Do you think Timothy has got the message yet?? One last time Paul urges him to turn his back on those who spread godless chatter. These guys claimed to have real knowledge but it was opposed to the truth of God's word.

Watch out for people who claim to have *'real knowledge'* or new understanding. Does what they say match up with the Bible?

PRAY ABOUT IT

Ask God to help you understand and hold on to the awesome truth of the gospel. Ask Him to help you recognise and stand against those who try to distort the truth.

→ TAKE IT FURTHER

For a quick review, go to page 124.

86 | Stars in your eyes

Have you ever seen a breathtaking starry sky or huge, awe-inspiring mountains? Something which made you realise how huge and magnificent God must be to have created all that?

👁 Read Psalm 8

ENGAGE YOUR BRAIN

▶ *How would you define 'majestic'?*

▶ *What evidence does David have that God is awesome and powerful?*

▶ *List the ways God shows He cares for people (v5–8):*

-
-
-
-

David has grasped two huge truths about God in this psalm and they are repeated in verses 1 and 9. God is majestic — He is the Creator, the Ruler, the King. But He is also **our** God — He cares for us and we have a personal relationship with Him. Doesn't that make you want to praise Him?

SHARE IT

The heavens are the work of God's fingers. The world around us shows God's amazing power. Do your non-Christian friends agree or do they think this world is a random accident? Why not chat to them about it?

▶ *The book of Hebrews tells us this psalm is also about Jesus. How does that come across in v4–8?*

Jesus, God's Son, became the perfect man. He ruled over God's creation and is now crowned with glory and honour. Jesus is our great King.

PRAY ABOUT IT

Use Psalm 8 to praise God for how awesome He is, to thank Him for caring for you and for sending His Son Jesus as the perfect King.

THE BOTTOM LINE

Our God is the King of all the earth.

→ TAKE IT FURTHER

Follow the stars to page 124.

87 | Compare and contrast

Ever noticed you look taller when standing next to someone short? Or that your grubby t-shirt looks much cleaner compared to your cruddy pair of jeans? Today David compares God's people with God's enemies.

👁 Read Psalm 9 v 1–12

ENGAGE YOUR BRAIN

▶ *How many phrases can you find that show that God is King and in control?*

▶ *What sort of king is He?*

▶ *Find a verse that shows how long God will be around for. Then find another one that shows how long his enemies last.*

David knew that God was the everlasting King, and he'd seen God's power and justice in defeating David's enemies. So what did he do? He gave thanks and told everyone by writing this song.

SHARE IT

Can you praise God by telling someone this week about some of the wonderful things He's done? The death and resurrection of Jesus is a pretty good place to start...

👁 Read verses 13–20

▶ *What is David asking God to do?*

▶ *What are the two outcomes? Look at:*
a) those who trust in God
b) those who forget Him.

God is known for His justice. He is the perfect and fair Judge. He will punish the wicked who reject Him, and He won't forget His people who are struggling and in need.

PRAY ABOUT IT

Pray for people you know who are not currently putting their trust in God. And pray for people you know who are in need, that God would show them His love and care.

→ TAKE IT FURTHER

Wander to wonders on page 124.

88 | Is anybody there?

Have you ever asked God why He lets bad things happen? Why He sometimes seems far away as if He doesn't care? You're not alone — the writer of this psalm had exactly the same questions.

👁 **Read Psalm 10 v 1–13**

ENGAGE YOUR BRAIN

▶ *Why does it seem as if God is a long way off?*

▶ *What do the wicked say or think about God? (v4, 11, 13)*

Such thoughts and questions seem reasonable. Does God notice corruption, persecution, and oppression? Is there even a God at all? The world is full of lies, cruelty and murder. Will God judge? The wicked seem to succeed and get away with evil.

👁 **Read verses 14–18**

▶ *Find a verse to answer each of these accusations...*
  • *God doesn't see:*

  • *God doesn't exist:*

  • *God won't punish evil:*

SHARE IT

Do any of your friends use these arguments? How could you answer them from this psalm and the rest of the Bible? (You might want to reflect on your answers and write them down, to help you get your head around them.)

PRAY ABOUT IT

Thank God that He does care about all the evil that goes on in this world. Thank Him that one day He will judge the world fairly. Thank Him that He will be King forever, long after the wicked are gone.

THE BOTTOM LINE

God sees, He will judge, He is the King forever.

➔ **TAKE IT FURTHER**

Need protection? Go to page 124.

89 Run for the hills

An increasingly anti-Christian society; TV, magazines and websites which ridicule Christians; friends and family who think you're stupid for believing in Christ. Wouldn't it be better to run for the hills and avoid all the hassle?

👁 Read Psalm 11 v1–3

ENGAGE YOUR BRAIN

▶ *What advice is David being offered? (v1b)*

▶ *Why? (v2–3)*

▶ *Why isn't he going to take it?*

Things may look hopeless — his enemies might well be deadly and destructive — but verses 4-7 explain David's reason for staying put.

👁 Read verses 4–7

▶ *Why did David have total confidence in the Lord?*

▶ *What does being 'righteous' mean (there's a clue in v1)?*

▶ *What is the amazing promise for those people? (v7)*

People were telling David to run from his enemies. But David was going nowhere. He had complete confidence in the Lord. He knew that God sees into people's hearts and judges them fairly. The Lord will destroy the wicked and violent (v5–6), but those who love and serve Him — the righteous — get to know God personally (v7). Incredible.

TALK IT THROUGH

Chat to a Christian friend. How can you remind each other that God is far more powerful than the world around us? What encouragement can you take from this psalm?

PRAY ABOUT IT

Ask God to help you turn to Him when you face opposition. Thank Him for His justice, protection and the promise of eternity with Him.

THE BOTTOM LINE

Find security in the Lord.

→ TAKE IT FURTHER

For more on everlasting safety and security, go to page 125.

90 | Speak no evil

'It's only a little white lie.'

'I was being economical with the truth'

'What they don't know won't hurt them.'

👁 **Read Psalm 12 v 1–4**

ENGAGE YOUR BRAIN

▷ *According to David, what is the big problem with the world?*

▷ *What are the different ways in which this problem shows itself?*

GET ON WITH IT

Ask yourself honestly if verse 2 applies to you.

• Do you talk about other people behind their backs?

• Is it easier to say what others want to hear than speak the truth?

• Would you lie to get out of trouble?

• Do you like to make yourself sound better than you really are?

Remind yourself of the truth of verse 3 and ask for God's help to change.

👁 **Read verses 5–8**

▷ *In contrast, what are God's words like? (v6)*

▷ *What is God's response to human wickedness? (v5, 7)*

▷ *What is the world's response?(v8)*

God's words are pure, perfect and completely trustworthy. So when He says He'll protect the weak and needy from the wicked, we can believe Him. God's people may get treated badly in this world, but one day they will be safe with God forever in eternity. And the wicked will be punished.

PRAY ABOUT IT

Thank God that He never lies, is totally trustworthy, and will keep His people safe forever.

THE BOTTOM LINE

Jesus is King!

→ **TAKE IT FURTHER**

The last *Take it Further* this issue is on page 125. Please don't cry.

TAKE IT FURTHER

If you want a little more at the end of each day's study, this is where you come. The TAKE IT FURTHER sections give you something extra. They look at some of the issues covered in the day's study, pose deeper questions, and point you to the big picture of the whole Bible.

GENESIS 12–17
Promises Promises

1 – GET UP AND GO

Read Hebrews 11 v 8–10. The New Testament book of Hebrews tells us that Abraham is a great model of faith in God.

▷ *Is there anything (wrong attitudes or habits) you need to leave behind as you set out to live God's way?*

▷ *What was Abraham ultimately looking forward to? (v10)?*

Abraham and his family waited for God to give them a new land to live in. But there would be more than just a country on earth for Abraham and all God's people. Eternal life with God in the heavenly city awaits all of His people!

2 – WHO DO YOU TRUST?

Abram had shown how much he trusted God by obeying the Lord's orders to move to a new country. But he failed the next test. We all mess up sometimes. Only Jesus always passed the test —
Read Luke 4 v 1–13.

Often in the Bible, people are tested after a real high point, so that they'll keep trusting Him. And that's true for us too. Ask God to help you be ready to face these hard times.

3 – TIME TO SPLIT

Check out Matthew 5 v 9 and James 3 v 18.
When Abram's and Lot's workers started to fight, Abram could have taken sides or demanded the best land for himself. Instead, he brought peace to the situation by generously letting Lot have first pick of the land.

▷ *Are there any situations in your life where you could be peacemaker?*
▷ *How can you bring peace to that situation?*

4 – SHOWING PROMISE

Check out these promises for God's people
Romans 10 v 9
John 3 v 16–18
Matthew 6 v 31–33
James 4 v 7–8
John 14 v 2–3

Pick one and learn it off by heart to encourage you when you most need it.

5 – LOT OF TROUBLE

Lot began living near Sodom, then moved into the godless city. The Bible warns us about getting too involved with people and situations that dishonour God. It's likely they'll change us rather than us changing them. **Take a look at Ephesians 4 v 17–24.**

6 – TWO FOR ONE OFFER

Check out **Hebrews 7 v 1–10 and 23–28** for the link between Melchizedek and Jesus. List three ways in which Jesus is the perfect high priest...

v25:

v26:

v27:

7 – GAME OF TWO HALVES

Read verse 6 again and then Romans 4 v 18–25
Righteous = being right with God, back in a true relationship with Him, where sin is not held against us. The result should be our right living for God

The right way to respond to God is **faith**. Faith isn't believing the unbelievable or having a warm fuzzy feeling. From Romans 4 v 18–25, write your own definition of *'faith'*.

8 – YOU'VE GOT ISHMAEL

Read verses 11–12
Ishmael would be a *'wild donkey'* — not an idiot, but independent and always battling people. The Arab people, descended from him, are often in conflict with the nation of Israel descended from Abram's son. God cared for Hagar and Ishmael even though they're not part of His promise to Abram. Today, God cares for people even though they're not Christians. **See Matthew 5 v 44–45.**

9 – LIFETIME GUARANTEE

Check out these verses about walking God's way:
Micah 6 v 8
1 John 1 v 5–7
Psalm 15

- ▶ What leaps out at you?
- ▶ What do you need to do about it?
- ▶ What do you need to talk to God about?

10 – PROMISE KEEPER

Old Testament prophets warned that circumcision wasn't enough on its own — people needed to trust God if they were to be right with Him. It gave special privileges (living among God's people in His land etc) but didn't guarantee being accepted by God. It wasn't automatic.

The prophets also said people needed to

'circumcise their hearts' — to change their attitude to God. From rebelling against Him to trust and obedience (Jeremiah 4 v 4).

Read Galatians 5 v 6

▷ *What matters far more than circumcision?*
▷ *How do you show that in your life?*

JOHN 6–8
Identity Parade

11 – JUST FOR STARTERS

In this miracle, John emphasises the huge amount of food Jesus provided for the people. In his Gospel, John keeps reminding us of all the things Jesus gave His people. Look up the following Bible bits and spot how John gives his readers examples of this greatness:

John 2 v 1–11
John 3 v 16
John 15 v 5–13
John 21 v 4–13
John 21 v 25

12 – WATER BREAK

Jesus had resisted the crowd making Him king, but He wanted His disciples to recognise that He was in control of the universe. He was the Creator who made the world and its laws, but His signs showed that He could alter those laws. No one else could do this, again proving that Jesus was God. Look back at some of the signs so far, and see how Jesus shows His Creator power:

John 2 v 6–11
John 4 v 46–54
John 5 v 1–14

13 – BREAD ROLES

Read verse 28. Jesus' hearers still think they've got the ability in themselves to do anything God requires. The boneheads.

▷ *What did they need to realise about eternal life?*

▷ *Know anyone who thinks they can earn their way to eternal life by being good?*

Spend time right now praying for them.

14 – BREAD OR ALIVE

Read more of Jesus' *'I AM'* claims in **John 6 v 35, 8 v 12, 10 v 7–9, 10 v 11, 11 v 25–26, 14 v 6 and 15 v 1–5.**

Now turn to Exodus 3 v 13–15.

▷ *So what was Jesus implying with His 'I AM' claims?*

16 – THE BIG CHOICE

Read verse 60. This was *'hard teaching'* because Jesus' hearers were more interested in stuff like food, miracles and power; they thought they had authority when it came to religious matters; they didn't like Jesus' claims to be superior to Moses; they found the talk of *'eating flesh'* offensive.

▷ *Can you see all of that lurking in v25–71?*

🔹 *Do you believe v68–69?*
🔹 *Will you still be following Jesus in, say, 5 years? Why?*

17 – WANTED: JESUS CHRIST

Read verses 6–8. Throughout His time on earth, Jesus made it clear that He would not do anything outside God's purpose for Him. He often said *'The right time (or 'hour') for me has not yet come'*. In Matthew 26 v 18 and in Mark 14 v 41, Jesus took this idea forward.

🔹 *What is the 'time' that Jesus always had in mind?*

18 – HEAVEN SENT

Read the full back-story behind today's argument. It's in **John 5 v 1–30**. Jot down anything that surprises you, confuses you or takes your breath away. Maybe you could talk to an older Christian about it.

19 – CHECK THE EVIDENCE

Have you been praying for friends and family who don't really understand who Jesus is? If it helps, list them below:

Now spend time praying for each of them individually, that they would see and accept the truth about Jesus.

20 – THIRST QUENCHER

Read verses 37–39 again. On the last day of the feast, loads of water was poured out as people prayed for God to send rain and and give them a great harvest. Jesus was saying: *'I fulfil all of this! If you want life–giving, heart–changing water, look no further'*.

Notice that Jesus hadn't given the Holy Spirit to believers yet (v39). To see what happened, read **Acts 2 v 1–47**.

21 – STAND UP, SPEAK OUT

For more on Nicodemus and Jesus, spend time in **John 3 v 1–21** and then **John 19 v 38–42**.

22 – SEXPLOSIVE

Let's face it, sin in the area of sex and relationships is often lurking nearby. This event reminds us: a) there is forgiveness; b) Christians need to work hard at staying pure and fighting temptation.

🔹 *What action do you need to take?*

HABAKKUK
God and the garbage

23 – TIME TO RANT

Look out for this pattern in Habakkuk:
1 v 2–4: Hab's first question
1 v 5–11: God's first reply
1 v 12–2 v 1: Hab's second question
2 v 2–20: God's second reply
3 v 1–19: Hab's song of response ----->

111

A prophet's job was chiefly to call God's people back to His *'covenant'* (His promise to give His people a great life when they obeyed His laws). But here the big shock (v2–4) is that it's Habakkuk who is calling *God* back to the covenant — *'Lord, you're a holy God who's promised to judge evil. Why aren't you doing anything?'*

▶ *Have you ever asked God questions beginning with 'Why?'*
▶ *What depth or honesty is there to your praying?*
▶ *Will you ask God to help Habakkuk (the book) change you?*

24 – GOD'S CHOSEN BULLIES

God was raising up a nation of bloodthirsty maniacs. It's a nice idea that God can bring good from evil, but is it really true?

Read Genesis 50 v 18-20

Joseph's brothers sold him for cash. Could anything be more heartless?
▶ *But what was God up to?*

Go to Acts 2 v 22-24

The crucifixion of an innocent man is impossibly evil.
▶ *But what was happening behind the scenes?*
▶ *Can you trust God to be working behind the scenes today?*

25 – THE BIG ISSUE

Life is unfair. Why does bad stuff happen? Is it all totally random? Or do people get what they deserve in life? Let's see how Jesus deals with this kind of question.
Read Luke 13 v 1-5.

▶ *Were the victims of these disasters at fault?*
▶ *What should our response be to this kind of tragedy? (v5)*
Jesus gives us a straight answer. Bad things are not necessarily sent as punishment on bad people.

Read Luke 13 v 6-9
▶ *Why did the vineyard owner want to cut his tree down?*
▶ *What advice did the gardener give?*
▶ *If people don't produce fruit, why don't they get chopped down straight away?*

God's answer to the world's evil is not to send instant punishment for every wrong act. Instead He has set a day in the future when things will get sorted. The day when Jesus will return as Judge. For more on this check **Matthew 13 v 24-30, 36-43**.

26 – WAITER WAITER
Read 2 Peter 3 v 3-7
▶ *What makes some people think Jesus won't return?*
▶ *What past events should they remember?*
▶ *We've been waiting for Jesus to return for nearly 2000 years. Should we be getting twitchy?*

Read 2 Peter 3 v 8–9

▶ *Why shouldn't a long wait for judgement day surprise us? (v8)*
▶ *What does it show us that God wants? (v9)*

It could happen at any time, and we need to be ready. But if the 'last day' is another thousand years away, it's because God wants more people to turn to Him.
▶ *What does that suggest we should be up to while we're waiting?*

27 – A WATERY END
Read Habakkuk 2 v 9–11. Verse 11 shows there's no escape when your success comes from mistreating others. It's like building a house with stolen bricks. The whole thing shouts **GUILTY!**

Read Proverbs 28 v 16
▶ *What's the right attitude to trampling on others for profit?*
▶ *What are your greatest achievements*
– in studies and qualifications?
– in talents and hobbies?
– in money and stuff?

Confess to your Father where you might have used others for your own advantage.
▶ *Is there anything you need to put right?*

28 – HOME-MADE GODS
If your belt lets you down in public, it's not a nice place to be. Being exposed can feel pretty uncomfortable. When people meet God in judgement, it won't be their wobbly bits causing them shame. It'll be

the secrets of their hearts.

Read Habakkuk 2 v 15–17
▶ *What's the payback for shaming others with drunkenness?*
▶ *What's the payback for violence and bloodshed?*
The drink God offers to Babylon is a cup of His anger — a common Bible picture for deserved punishment. As God has already made clear, He knows everything this evil nation has been up to. And He knows about us too. **Check out Hebrews 4 v 13.**

Stop where you are. Let God search the corners of your heart. Admit to Him every secret sin. And know again His forgiveness through Jesus. Use **Psalm 139 v 23–24** to get started.

29 – LIVING IN THE PAST
Read Colossians 2 v 15
▶ *What does the victory of the cross do to the forces of evil?*
The devil is called the accuser (Revelation 12 v 10). That is, he tries to hold our failures against us. But Jesus' death did away with the rule book. So there's nothing to accuse us with. The devil is an enemy with no weapons! Hopeless!

If you feel the weight of past sins squeezing the joy out of you, just remember the cross, and that Satan is finished. Thank God today for His total victory!

30 – THE HAPPY HABIT

How could Hab say v17–18? Talking of God with joy when there was no sign of God's help in a time of urgent need? Had Hab lost his marbles?

▷ *Having read chapters 1 and 2, why is Hab not stupid to speak like this?*

▷ *How do you cope with difficult circumstances? By complaining, ignoring them, gritting your teeth?*

▷ *Will you learn, like Hab, to find joy in God through hard times?*

That's all from Habakkuk. Someone who took his hard questions to God and found answers that blew him away. Answers that drastically enlarged his view of God and His work in the world.

▷ *What has the book of Habakkuk done for you?*

GENESIS 18–25

31 – PROMISES PROMISES

Sarah thought it was too late — there would be no answer to her prayer for a child. She doubted God's promise. But God showed He was fully in control and would give her a son in His own timing (v14). Sarah's response (and God's reply to her) reminds us of prayers which seem to go unanswered by God.

▷ *What do we need to remember about God? Maybe something you learnt from Habakkuk?*

▷ *What should be our attitude while we wait for answers?*

32 – GOD IN CONVERSATION

Check out James 2 v 23. Abraham was God's friend. Because of Jesus' death on the cross, all Christians can call themselves God's friends. And we can talk intimately with Him, just as Abraham did.

For tips on talking with God, try **Matthew 6 v 5–15.**

33 – LOT IN A HOT SPOT

God says that homosexual sex isn't part of His plan: **Leviticus 18 v 22**
Romans 1 v 26–27
1 Corinthians 6 v 9
But that's not an excuse for anti-gay hate. God loves all sinners and wants them to live His way, whatever the sin. We need to show God's love to people, even if we disagree with their lifestyle.

34 – WORD OF WARNING

Read Luke 17 v 28–33

▷ *How serious is it to ignore God's warnings?*

▷ *How important is it that people realise the consequences of rejecting God?*

▷ *So what are you going to do about it?*

▷ *Who will you tell about God's judgement and His rescue through Jesus?*

▷ *How will you do it?*

35 – WHAT A MESS

We'll let you work out for yourself what the Bible says about alcohol…
Psalm 104 v 14–15
Proverbs 20 v 1

Proverbs 23 v 20–21
John 2 v 1–11
Ephesians 5 v 18
Galatians 5 v 19–21

36 – OLD HABITS DIE HARD

A prophet had a special relationship with God — saying what God wanted him to say and praying for others. Yet Abimelech acted in a more godly way than God's prophet, Abraham.

▷ *Why do you think non-Christians often seem better at doing the right thing than Christians?*
▷ *What behaviour do you need to change?*

37 – ABE'S BABE

**Read Isaiah 54 v 1
and Psalm 126**
When God shows His faithfulness to us, and to His promises, the only fitting response is joy. As Christians, we often forget how amazing it is that God is faithful to His word. The only apt response to such grace can be joy, laughter, thanks and praise.

38 – OUTCAST OUTCRY

The Lord heard Ishmael crying and rescued him. **Read Psalm 40.**
▷ *What was David's past experience? (v1–2)*
▷ *How does he feel now? (v2–3)*
▷ *How is this psalm a picture of the Christian life?*
▷ *Anything you recognise from your own life?*

▷ *What does this psalm remind you about God?*

39 – OH WELL

Abraham is a man who has been promised the land, doesn't own it yet, but lives in it. This means he's in danger. In this situation, one response is to act in a cowardly way by lying and cheating (as he did in chapter 20, pretending Sarah was his sister). Another response is to wait for God to keep His promises, and to act as God does, showing kindness to the people in the land. That's what happened here in chapter 21.

▷ *When you're in a tricky situation, do you take the easy way out, or do you try with all your strength to treat people fairly and live God's way?*

40 – THE TOUGHEST TEST

Abraham had to trust God to keep His promise (about blessing the nations through his son Isaac). He was prepared to put Isaac to death, even thought it would appear to spell the end of the promise.

Read Hebrews 11 v 17–19
As God tests our faith, we're to trust His promises.
▷ *What normally happens to your trust in God when things work out worse than expected?*

Read James 2 v 20–24
Abraham obeyed what God said, even though it was ridiculously tough. We may not be tested like this, but the challenge

for us is to read the Bible and do exactly what God says. Without making excuses, ignoring it or taking the easiest option.

41 – IN THE NICK OF TIME
One reason why God tested Abraham in this way was to give a picture of another father who sacrificed his own son.

Read 1 John 4 v 9–10

▶ *Have you accepted this amazing gift?*

▶ *Have you turned to Jesus and trusted Him to forgive you for all your sin?*

Spend time talking to God about your answer and how it makes you feel.

And for a family update, check out the verses we missed: **Genesis 22 v 20–24**.

43 – THIGH WILL BE DONE
Read Philippians 4 v 6

▶ *What should you do if you're worrying?*

▶ *What things should you bring before God in prayer?*

▶ *How should you bring these requests to God?*

Try putting this great verse into practice right now.

44 – SHE'S THE ONE
Want to keep track of God your answering prayers? Make a **prayer diary** — it's obvious really. Grab a notebook and keep track of what you pray about, with the dates next to your prayers. At the end of each month, look back over your prayers and prepare to be surprised...

46 – END OF THE ROAD
Abraham never saw God's big three promises fulfilled in his lifetime:

1. His family have yet to receive a whole land to live in.
2. And though God gave Abraham a son in his old age, he didn't live to see his family grow into a great nation, as promised.
3. Abraham had been blessed by God, but never saw *'all nations'* be blessed by his family.

Despite all this, Abraham lived a life showing how much he trusted God's promises. He kept trusting, believing and clinging to God — a great example to us. We need to show such faith. Sometimes eternal life seems a long way off — but it's a certain promise for God's people.
Read this brilliant passage — Hebrews 12 v 1–3

JOHN 8–10

47 – LIGHT CONVERSATION
Read Psalm 27 v 1 and John 1 v 4–5
In the Old Testament, it's God who is called *'light'*. Now it's Jesus taking this title. And it's light for the world — not just those in Israel. Shocker! It's light that produces life. Eternal life.

49 – FINDING FREEDOM
▶ *What would you say to a friend who wanted to follow Jesus?*

Got your answer? Now review verses 31–32. Does this change your answer? Notice that Jesus wasn't interested in big numbers of converts if they weren't genuine believers. So He slapped down the cost of identifying with Him. It's not an easy life, following Jesus.

▶ *Are you prepared to stick with Jesus, whatever happens?*
▶ *Honestly?*

Read Galatians 3 v 6–9
▶ *Who can truly call themselves Abraham's children? (v7, 9)*

Read verses 53–55
Jesus wasn't just bigging Himself up. God the Father was the one who was revealing Jesus' glory, showing everyone who Jesus really was. These people claimed to know God, but they didn't know Him at all.

God the Father is the key to knowing who Jesus is. Jesus is the one the Father promised to send into the world. He kept His promise.

On spare paper, jot down exactly who you think Jesus is. Not what you think you *should* write, but what you genuinely believe about Jesus. Pray about your answers and about the way you'll respond to Jesus and who He is.

Read verses 1–3
Are sin and suffering linked? If we lie, will we suddenly get a nasty disease? Well, the Bible says they *are* linked. Adam and Eve's sin brought suffering into the world. But that doesn't mean that each thing we suffer is because of a particular sin.

Here the man's blindness was not caused by his sin. His suffering was actually used to bring glory to God! Amazing.

▶ *What difficult questions do people ask you about your faith?*
▶ *How would you rate your answers?*
▶ *How could you improve them?*
▶ *Any older Christians you could talk to about this stuff?*
▶ *The ex-blind man didn't know much about Jesus. He just said what he knew. How can that encourage you?*

Read verses 28–29 again
They were so committed to being disciples of Moses and keeping all the Jewish laws, they let it take over their lives. These laws became more important than actually living God's way. It made them blind to the reality that Jesus was the Messiah — the one sent by God to rescue them from slavery to sin.

▶ *How might we fall into the same trap?*
▶ *Do we ever put traditions ahead of what God actually wants?*

TAKE IT FURTHER

▶ *Ever doubt that someone's really a Christian because they don't do things the same way as you?*

55 – BLIND FAITH

**Read Daniel 7 v 13–14
and Revelation 1 v 12–18**

▶ *Jot down what you learn from these verses about Jesus, the Son of Man.*
▶ *Does it alter your view of Him at all?*
▶ *How?*

56 – FEELING SHEEPISH

Read Psalm 23

▶ *What does the Lord do for His sheep?*
v1:

v2:

v3:

▶ *What comfort can Christians take in dark times? (v4)*
▶ *When life is tough, why is the future still bright for believers? (v6)*

57 – GATE EXPECTATIONS

Read John 14 v 6

▶ *What's the only way to the Father?*
▶ *What extra things do some people say you need to be right with God?*
▶ *What would you say to someone who reckons you need Jesus plus other stuff to be a Christian?*
▶ *How would you back up your answer?*

58 – FLOCK TACTICS

Read Revelation 7 v 9–10

▶ *What's amazing about God's people?*

Read Matthew 28 v 18–20

▶ *What does Jesus command His disciples?*
▶ *How does that challenge you?*
▶ *What are you going to do about it?*

59 – LIFE-CHANGING WORDS

There's been loads of sheep-related teaching over the last few days. Read all the way through **John 10 v 1–30**, noting:

– *What Jesus claimed about Himself*

– *What Jesus claimed about His Father*

– *What Jesus claimed about His followers*

– *The people's reactions.*

HAGGAI
Home truths

61 – HOME IMPROVEMENT

To see how it all hangs together, read all of Haggai in one go.

If you want to read more about God's people returning to Jerusalem, read the books of **Ezra** and **Nehemiah**, who got the re-building of Jerusalem's walls going. Also check out **Zechariah**, who was a prophet at a similar time to Haggai.

118

Read Haggai 1 v 12

What does it mean to fear the Lord? It means to show awe and respect for the Lord. To recognise that it's God who is in control of EVERYTHING.

When people truly fear the Lord, they have a desire to please Him, like these guys in Haggai. We please God by showing obedience to Him (just as Abraham did when God told him to sacrifice Isaac).

Read Psalm 111 v 10

To fear God is to love Him more than yourself, your family, your friends. When people fear the Lord, they're being wise.

Read John 2 v 18–22

Jesus is the new temple — the place where we meet God. Our verses today in Haggai are just a tiny glimpse of the amazing future still to come.

Read Revelation 21 v 22–27

Check out **Hebrews 9 v 11–14** for the ultimate sin antidote.

▷ *What was incredible about the sacrifice Jesus offered? (v12)*
▷ *What did it achieve? (v12b)*
▷ *Which words in verse 12 show it's effective for ever?*
▷ *What should Jesus death for us encourage us to do? (v14)*

As we live as Christians, making God our top priority, we look forward to God's gift of eternal life and the life to come. But it's not all future — what about NOW?

Read Romans 8 v 12–17

Some of the benefits we get right now from living for God:

• knowing that God is our Father (v15)
• no need for fear as we approach God (v15)
• our changed lives are evidence of God at work in lives (v16)
• the certainty of our inheritance — living forever with God (v17)
• sufferings too (v17).

1 TIMOTHY

Holy Housework

Read more warnings from Paul in **Acts 20 v 28–31**

▷ *Who appoints church leaders? (v28)*
▷ *Why is God's family (the church) so special? (v28)*
▷ *What dangers do churches face? (v29–30)*

Take time to pray for church leaders you know, that they would fight false teaching and serve God faithfully.

67 – POINT OF LAW

To read the Old Testament in one year, try this reading plan. Make sure you read the New Testament alongside it.

Week 1: Genesis 1-10, Psalm 1-3, Isaiah 1–4, Proverbs 1
Week 2: Gen 11–20, Psalms 4–6, Isaiah 5–8, Proverbs 2
3: Gen 21–30, Ps 7–9, Isaiah 9–12, Prov 3
4: Gen 31–40, Ps 10–12, Isa 13–16, Prov 4
5: Gen 41–50, Ps 13–15, Isa 17–20, Prov 5
6: Exod 1–10, Ps 16–18, Isa 21–24, Prov 6
7: Exo 11–20, Ps 19–21, Isa 25–28, Prov 7
8: Exo 21–30, Ps 22–24, Isa 29–32, Prov 8
9: Exo 31–40, Ps 25–27, Isa 33–36, Prov 9
10: Lev 1–10, Ps 28–30, Isa 37–41, Prov10
11. Lev 11–20, Ps 31–33, Is 42–46, Prov11
12. Lev 21–27, Ps 34–36, Is 47–51, Prov 12, Numbers 1–2
13. Num 3–12, Ps 37–39, Is 52–56, Prov13
14. Num 13–22, Ps 40–42, Is 57–61, Prov14
15. Num 23–32, Ps 43–45, Is 62–66, Prov15
16. Num 33–36, Deuteronomy 1–6, Psalms 46–48, Jeremiah 1–4, Prov 16
17. Deu 7–16, Ps 49–51, Jer 5–8, Prov 17
18. Deu 17–26, Ps 52–54, Jer 9–12, Prov18
19. Deu 27–34, Ps 55–57, Jer 13–16, Prov19
20. Joshua 1–10, Ps 58–60, Jer 17–20, Prov 20
21. Jos 11–20, Ps 61–63, Jer 21–24, Prov21
22. Joshua 21–24, Judges 1–6, Ps 64–66, Jer 25–28, Prov 22
23. Jud 7–16, Ps 67–68, Jer 29–32, Prov 23
24. Judges 17–21, Ruth 1–4, Ps 69–70, Jer 33–36, Prov 24
25. 1 Samuel 1–10, Ps 71–73, Jer 37–40, Prov 25
26. 1 Sam 11–20, Ps 74–76, Jer 41–44, Prov 26
27. 1 Sam 21–31, Ps 77–78, Jer 45–48, Prov 27
28. 2 Sam 1–10, Ps 79-81, Jer 49–52, Prov 28
29. 2 Sam 11–20, Ps 82–84, Prov 29, Lamentations 1–5
30. 2 Sam 21–24, 1 Kings 1–6, Ps 85–87, Ezekiel 1–4, Prov 30
31. 1Kgs 7–16, Ps 88–89, Eze 5–8, Prov31
32. 1Kgs 17–22, 2 Kgs 1–4, Ps 90–92, Ezekiel 9–12, Ecclesiastes 1
33. 2Kgs 5–14, Ps 93–95, Eze 13–16, Ecc 2
34. 2Kgs 15–25, Ps 96–98, Eze17–20, Ecc 3
35. 1 Chronicles 1–10, Ps 99-101, Ezek 21–24, Ecc 4
36. 1 Chron 11–20, Ps 102–4, Eze 25-28, Ecc 5
37. 1 Chron 21–29, Ps 105–6, Eze 29–32, Ecc 6
38. 2 Chron 1–10, Ps 107–8, Eze 33–36, Ecc 7
39. 2 Chron 11–20, Ps 109–11, Eze 37–40 Ecc 8
40. 2 Chron 21–30, Ps 112–14, Eze 41–44 Ecc 9
41. 2 Chron 31–36, Ps 115–18, Ezek 45–48, Ecc 10
42. Ezra 1–10, Ps 119, Daniel 1–4, Ecc 11
43. Nehemiah 1–13, Ps 120–123, Dan 5–8 Ecc 12
44. Esther 1–10, Ps 124–6, Dan 9–12
45. Job 1–8, Ps 127–9, Hosea 1-4, Song of Songs 1-2
46. Job 9–18, Ps 130–132, Hos 5–8, Song 3
47. Job 19–28, Ps 133–5, Hos 9–12, Song 4
48. Job 29–42, Ps 136–8, Hos 13–14, Song5

49. Zech 1–6, Ps 139–41, Joel 1–3, Song 6
50. Amos 1–9, Ps 142–4, Zech 7–10, Song 7–8
51. Jonah 1–4, Micah 1–7, Ps 145–150, Zech 11–14, Obadiah 1
52. Nahum 1–3, Habakkuk 1–3, Zeph 1–3, Mal 1–4, Haggai 1–2

68 – AMAZING GRACE

Want to read about Paul becoming a Christian? **Go to Acts 8 v 1–3, then Acts 9 v 1–31.**

Read 1 Timothy 1 v 15

Paul doesn't say *'of whom i **was** the worst'*, but *'I **am** the worst.'*

▶ *How does this encourage Christians who feel they're never good enough to be used by God?*

▶ *How does it challenge those who look down on others?*

▶ *What does it tell us about the ongoing Christian life?*

69 – FIGHTING TALK

Read verse 20

Hymenaeus and Alexander had given up on their faith in Christ. By handing them *'over to Satan'* Paul probably means that they were thrown out of the church so they couldn't do even more harm to other Christians. They'd be excluded from the church until they repented of their behaviour or false teaching.

70 – PRAY FOR EVERYONE

Read verse 8

Paul's not saying that prayer is only for men. And he's not saying you have to pray with your hands in the air — that's probably just how they did it back then. Paul is saying that everyone everywhere must **pray**. They should pray about difficult situations instead of resorting to anger, arguments and aggression.

▶ *What do you need to pray about?*

71 –CONTROVERSIAL STUFF

This section of the Bible sometimes gets used to answer loads of questions about feminism and women's roles. Paul was addressing a specific problem — the teaching role in church. So you can't apply these verses to all situations. Keep the verses in context.

Read verse 14

Paul doesn't put the blame entirely on Eve for the fall (when sin came into the world — Genesis 3). In Romans 5, Paul says the responsibility for sin is Adam's. Eve was deceived by the serpent, but Adam disobeyed God knowingly.

Get chatting with others. 1 Tim 2 needs discussing!

72 –LEADING EXAMPLE

Rewrite the description of a church leader (verses 2–7) in your own words. Then spend time praying for your church's leaders — that they will grow to be more and more like your description.

73 – SERVING SUGGESTIONS

Read verse 16

Again, Paul got all excited about Jesus and burst into spontaneous praise. It's like a mini worship song to Jesus. A super-fast summary of Jesus' life on earth. Look up the Bible bits that talk about these different aspects of Jesus' life:

"He appeared in a body' — **John 1 v 14**
'vindicated (shown to be right)
by the Spirit' — **Matthew 3 v 16**
'seen by angels' — **Mark 1 v 13,**
Luke 22 v 39–44
'was preached among the nations —
Matthew 28 v 19–20
'believed in the world' — **Acts 2 v 38–41**
'taken up in glory' — **Mark 16 v 19**

74 – DON'T EAT THAT, DON'T MARRY HIM

Read verse 1

▶ How much do you analyse teaching or advice you receive to check if it's from the Bible?
▶ Which older Christians can you ask about anything you're unsure about?
Why not arrange to meet one of them, and compile a list of questions you have.

Read verse 4

▶ How could you make sure you appreciate God's creation more?
▶ At mealtimes, do you thank God from your heart, or just say the same old thing that doesn't mean much?

75 – BODY BUILDING

Read verses 9–10

This is Paul's third *'trustworthy saying'* — things he really wants Tim to take on board. Check out the other two:
1 Timothy 1 v 15, 1 Timothy 3 v 1
And two more in other letters by Paul:
2 Timothy 2 v 11–13 and Titus 3 v 4–8

▶ Which one of these sayings do you really need to take to heart?
Why not write it out and stick it on your wall? And learn it off by heart.

76 – TOO MUCH TOO YOUNG?

Read verse 12

Tim might have been anything up to the age of 35, but:
▶ What can young people do for God that older Christians are less able to do?

Read verse 14

God's gifts to us require us to actually use them. Tim was to use his spiritual gifts and abilities as best he could.
▶ How will you serve God with what He's given you?

Read verse 16

What a great motto for Christians. We should make sure that our lives and beliefs match up to what Jesus requires of us.
▶ What areas of Christian lifestyle are hard for young people?
▶ What Christian beliefs do you find it difficult to hold on to?

77 – FAMILY FORTUNES
Read Mark 3 v 31–35
- Who is part of Jesus' family?
- What does it mean to treat other Christians as your brothers, sisters, father and mother?

Make a list of at least six people in your church (or C.U. or youth group) who you don't like or haven't got to know.
- *How can you pray for them?*
- *How can you show some practical care for them as members of Christ's family?*

78 – WIDOW OF OPPORTUNITY
Read Psalm 146
- What comfort is there here for the poor and lonely Christian?
- What does this psalm tell you about God?

79 – MERRY WIDOWS
Read Acts 6 v 1–7
- What were the problems? (v1, 2)
- What was the solution? (v3)
- What was the result? (v7)

The most important thing was to make sure that the gospel spread and people became Christians (v7). But it was also important that those in need were looked after.

- *What can you do to share the truth about Jesus more?*
- *How can you help people who are in need?*

80 – DOUBLE HONOUR
- How do your attitudes towards Christian leaders need to change?
- What positive things can you do to support and encourage them?

Why not write emails, letters or make phone calls thanking and encouraging your church leaders? Go on, what are you waiting for?

81 – WORK IT OUT
Check out other stuff Paul wrote about slaves and their masters:

Ephesians 6 v 5–9
Colossians 3 v 22 – 4 v 1
The book of Philemon

Now spend time praying for:
- people who have authority over you
- Christian mates who get a hard time from their bosses
- Christian teachers you know.

82 – LOVE OF MONEY
Find it hard to be content with what you've got? Read these other Bible passages on the subject — writing down what you learn about God and what you can do to be more content.

Ecclesiastes 5 v 10–20
Hebrews 13 v 5
Matthew 6 v 24–34
Philippians 4 v 10–13

- How should a Christian's attitude to money and possessions differ from everybody else's?

83 – FIGHTING TALK

**Read verse 13 and then
John 18 v 28 – 19 v 16**

The ultimate reason why we should keep
going in the faith is because Jesus did.
He did so to the very end — even in front
of Pilate when an opportunity came to
deny everything, walk free and escape
crucifixion. Thank God, Jesus didn't
walk away.

84 – REAL RICHES

Read 2 Corinthians 9 v 6–15

▶ *What do v6–7 teach us about giving?*
▶ *What's the promise for those who give
   sacrificially? (v10–11)*
▶ *What does giving generously lead to?
   (v12–14)*
▶ *How will you change what you do
   with your money and possessions?*

85 – FINAL WORDS

Go back over 1 Timothy and work out
what its main themes have been: eg the
need for proper Bible teaching in church.
Choose at least two others. Then thank
God for everything you've learnt in
1 Timothy. Be specific. And pray for all
the stuff you've been challenged about.

▶ *What would you say to recommend
   1 Timothy to a friend?*

PSALMS

86 – STARS IN YOUR EYES

Read Hebrews 2 v 5–9

▶ *How does this build on Psalm 8?*
▶ *Why is Jesus now crowned with glory
   and honour? (v9)*
▶ *Why was Jesus' death so special?*

87 – COMPARE AND CONTRAST

Read verse 1

▶ *Any idea what 'wonders' David might
   have in mind?*

Look at this major event the Israelites
could look back on and see God at work;
Exodus 14 v 10–31, 15 v 11.

See God's wonders in David's life:
2 Samuel 5 v 17–25.

For us, we can look back to the wonders
Jesus performed. The Gospels and Acts are
full of them. **See Acts 2 v 22–24.**

Now you've got loads more things to
thank and praise God for...

88 – IS ANYBODY THERE?

As in Psalm 9, David's in a frightening
situation. But he knows bigger truths he
can trust in, and a bigger person he can
call out to who will hear and help.

▶ *Is this your experience too?*
▶ *So what will God protect us from?*
Well, not always from physical attack
or harm in this world. Christians are
promised that they'll suffer in this world

(and they may be physically attacked). The protection the psalm writer is talking about is protection from God's eternal judgement and destruction on the last day. That's what we're safe from in Jesus. In the end, it's the best security we have.

That's what Paul said in **Romans 8 v 31–39**. Read it.
▶ *Can you say all that for yourself?*

89 – RUN FOR THE HILLS
If we take refuge in the Lord by putting our trust in Christ's death and resurrection, then the promise of verse 7 is for us too.

Read Revelation 21 v 22 – 22 v 5
▶ *What things won't be in God's new kingdom?*
   v22:

   v23:

   v25:

   v27:

   22 v 3:

▶ *So who and what will be there?*
   21 v 22–23:

   22 v 1–2:

   22 v 3–4:

▶ *Who will see God's face? (v3–4)*

▶ *What kind of life will believers have in God's new kingdom?*

90 – SPEAK NO EVIL
The Bible has lots to say about words, lies, deception and boasting:

Psalm 34 v 11–14
Psalm 141 v 3
Proverbs 6 v 16–19
Proverbs 12 v 17–22
Proverbs 13 v 3
James 3 v 3–12

engage wants to hear from YOU!

▷ How can we make engage even better?
▷ Share experiences of God at work in your life
▷ Any questions you have about the Bible or the Christian life?

Email us — **engage@thegoodbook.com**

Or use the space below to write us a real letter. You can post it to:

engage 37 Elm Road, New Malden, Surrey, KT3 3HB, UK.

In the next **engage**...

John All signs point to Jesus
Genesis Dreamer drama
Zechariah Restoration work
Micah The King and I
Plus: Philemon, Death, other religions and the lowdown on God's Son

---

Order **engage** now!

Make sure you order the next issue of engage. Or, even better, grab a one-year subscription to make sure engage plops through your letterbox as soon as it's out.

Visit www.thegoodbook.com
Or phone us in the UK on 0845 225 0880